THE MODEL RAILROADER'S GUIDE TO
COAL
RAILROADING

TONY KOESTER

KALMBACH
BOOKS

Acknowledgments

I am indebted to many individuals for their help with this book, most of whom are credited in the captions. Among those who made special efforts to provide information and photos are Chuck Bohi, Jim Boyd, Mike Brestel, Eric Brooman, Joe Collias, Sharon Deckard, Paul Dolkos, Jerry Glow, Jeff Halloin, Mark Hemphill, Eric Hirsimaki, Frank Hodina, Kevin Keefe, Lloyd Keyser, Jeff Kraker, Bill Miller, Bob Penin, Bill Raia, Ted Richardson, John Roberts, Stan Rydarowitz, Jim Singer, Mark Vaughan, John Waite, John Wilkes, Jeff Wilson, and Chuck Yungkurth.

Tony Koester
Newton, N.J.
April 2006

On the cover
Clockwise from upper left: A scene on David Stewart's freelanced Appalachian & Ohio O scale layout, which was featured in May 2006 *Model Railroader* (Bob Sobol photo); an eastbound Rio Grande coal train easing through Glenwood Springs, Colo., in 1985; and the Baltimore & Ohio's coal marshalling yard at Keyser, W.Va., in 1976 (prototype photos by Tony Koester). Back cover: For photo credits and captions (from top to bottom) see pages 63, 53, 36, and 47.

Printed in China

10 09 08 07   2 3 4 5

Visit our Web site at
http://kalmbachbooks.com
Secure online ordering available

Publisher's Cataloging-In-Publication Data
(Prepared by The Donohue Group, Inc.)

Koester, Tony.
   The model railroader's guide to coal railroading / by Tony Koester.

   p.: ill., maps ; cm.

   ISBN-13: 978-0-89024-668-9
   ISBN-10: 0-89024-668-8

1. Railroads – Models. 2. Railroads – Models – Design and construction.
3. Railroads – United States – Freight-cars – History. 4. Coal – Transportation – History. I. Title. II. Title: Coal railroading

TF197 .K64 2006
625.1/9

CONTENTS

Introduction

Tony Koester

From a distance, it's just "coal." But get up close and personal and you'll find that a carload of coal is as unique as a carload of automobiles or grain or television sets, a specific commodity headed for a picky customer. Some of the black oceans of coal that roll out of the bountiful Appalachians are gathered here at Keyser, W.Va., on the former Baltimore & Ohio (CSX today).

One of the first long auto trips my family took was an early 1950s venture into the Cumberland Mountains. For a pre-teen boy who was born and raised in corn country, visiting this segment of the Appalachian chain was an eye-opener. It was like encountering an ocean, except here the ocean's blue-gray was replaced by an undulating sea of well-worn green mountains and freight classification yards filled with countless hopper cars brimming with tons of black coal. I was impressed!

From Lionel to lake coal

A basic-black Norfolk & Western hopper with magnetically operating hopper-bay doors soon joined the roster of my Lionel O-27 railroad. My railroad and I were now officially in the business of hauling coal! Little did I know then that a single open hopper would one day be replaced by a sea of HO scale hoppers hauling scale ton upon ton of black diamonds out of the Appalachians as "tide coal" to tidewater ports, and as "lake coal" to power plants and steel mills along the Great Lakes.

In the late 1940s, hoppers made up more than a quarter of the nation's freight-car fleet. Even in the 21st century, more than 40 percent of the tonnage that rolls over American rails is coal. Fully 70 percent of that coal comes from Wyoming, West Virginia, and Kentucky. Twenty percent of the coal originates in Wyoming, 95 percent of that in the Powder River Basin. Clearly, the slump in coal production predating the energy crisis of the 1970s is over. What is no longer burned in home furnaces and steam-locomotive fireboxes goes to electric-power generating stations instead.

If asked to write down the names of "coal railroads," odds are that many modelers would think first of the Norfolk & Western, Southern, Chesapeake & Ohio, Virginian, Clinchfield, Pennsylvania, Western Maryland, Baltimore & Ohio, or Louisville & Nashville, among others – today, Norfolk Southern and CSX. Those with a western perspective might list the Rio Grande and Union Pacific or, in recent times, Burlington Northern Santa Fe, which serves the vast coalfields around Gillette, Wyoming.

But don't forget that considerable coal was and is buried beneath the Midwest and South. Texas now ranks fifth in coal production behind Wyoming, West Virginia, Kentucky, and

Photographs and books about coal railroading, like coal, take time and some "mining" to produce. Here the author's 1967 Chevy station wagon serves as a raised promontory during one of many trips he and friends from New Jersey took into the coalfields in the 1970s.

Pennsylvania. Drive through southern Indiana, as I recently did, and you'll see sprawling coal mines served by regional railroads such as the Indiana Rail Road and the Indiana Southern. The Illinois Central worked the mines of Kentucky, and the Burlington and Wabash and Chicago & Illinois Midland and even the Milwaukee Road, among others, made a nice living in the Midwestern coalfields.

In 96 pages, I couldn't begin to explore each of these fascinating operations in depth or provide detailed coverage about modeling them. Instead, I sought out interesting vignettes about each region to share with you. *The Model Railroader's Guide to Coal Railroading* is therefore a sampler, an idea book, a toehold from which I hope you'll be inspired to explore the concepts behind moving coal from mine to market, and then to model this fascinating

activity in your favorite scale.

We'll start by whetting your appetite with David P. Morgan's classic tale of how the Chesapeake & Ohio moved coal from the mine head to a ship waiting at an Atlantic seaport back in 1956. We'll then travel back much farther in time—hundreds of millions of years—to see how coal was formed and where it was deposited. We'll visit the company towns where miners and their families lived and discuss each of the major coal regions from the East Coast to the West, and we'll review where the coal went: ocean, lake, or river ports; steel mills; power plants; and even small retail coal yards. Finally, we'll discuss motive power and how the movement of heavy coal trains enhances model railroad operations.

I think you'll find it a fascinating journey.

W.A. Akin, Jr.

ONE

Above: Using her steam twice, Mallet 1498 – built by Schenectady in 1923 – shoves hoppers 134594 and 47859 to the mine. Almost two decades later, in May 1975, the author and Jim Boyd photographed the Scarlet Shifter's motive power – by then, a pair of Geeps – on the same trestle (opposite page).

Before we discuss how coal came to be and where it can be found across the North American continent and before we review examples of coal railroading in various regions and ways to model it, I want to share with you a fascinating primer on coal railroading titled "Tide 470." This is the story of two hoppers, Chesapeake & Ohio 134594 and 47859, as they traveled 512 miles and 96 hours in the summer of 1955 to help the C&O move coal from the mountains to a ship at tidewater. It was written by David P. Morgan, former editor of *Trains* magazine and author of the "Steam in Indian Summer" series, illustrated by Dr. Philip R. Hastings. The article originally appeared in the April 1956 issue of *Trains*. "Tide 470" is reprinted here together with several of W.A. (Bill) Akin's evocative photographs from the original article.

Tony Koester and Jim Boyd

I designed and operated my HO scale Allegheny Midland RR based largely on what I learned about coal railroading from David P. Morgan's informative piece. I hope you find it equally inspiring.
— *Tony Koester*

Coal's journey

Last year, the greatest coal carrier of them all, Chesapeake & Ohio, hauled 61.6 million tons of it away from on-line mines in a fleet of 62,000 company hoppers and gondolas. Awesome figures, these – perhaps not even comprehensible to the statisticians who compile them. To place such an enormous traffic in focus, *Trains* selected just 512 miles and 96 hours, 10 minutes out of the lives of two of C&O's hoppers as they rolled 121.8 tons of West Virginia bituminous from a tipple on Cow Creek to the dumpers at tidewater. This is their story.

Danville, W.Va., is one of those places that must be duplicated uncountable times in the perpetual mountains of the greatest coal-producing state in the Union. It is simply a yard filled with black

C&O hoppers, half of them loaded with coal and bound for the main line (33 rail miles away down Little Coal River) and half empty and slated for nearby mines. There's a yard office, an engine terminal, Mrs. Ballard's rooming house just across U.S. 119, a population of 544, and an overcast blended of mist and locomotive smoke in equal parts. Danville's a working town, no pretensions allowed. It's where the august 2-8-4s arrive with empties from the outside world, nod briefly to the chunky Mallets that work the pits, then storm back to civilization with the stuff that heats homes, forges steel, and generates power.

Transients are Danville's stock in trade, and on the morning of June 2, 1955, a couple of them are 50-ton hoppers 134594 and 47859. The sun has barely crawled over the ridges when these cars and a sizable number of their brethren are trundling out of Danville behind the Vanderbilt tank of a compound 2-6-6-2 as Extra 1498 East, known locally as the Barrett Shifter. The empties coil deeper and deeper into the backwoods on

a Pond Fork Subdivision where a boxcar is a rarity and passenger service is nonexistent. Finally, 22½ miles from home base, the Schenectady articulated cuts off hoppers 134594 and 47859 and clanks back around the leg of a wye at Barrett, across a timber trestle, and up a stiff, curving grade to Wharton No. 2, a modern tipple operated by Eastern Gas & Fuel Associates.

Multi-storied, glass-windowed, metal-sided, smoke-belching Wharton No. 2 is as far removed from the era of pick-and-shovel and blind-mule mining as steam from diesel. Even as the Barrett Shifter came up the valley, the coal for its empties was being mechanically dug and hoisted to the surface. Then, in the preparation plant, the coal was dumped into surge bins, thence into the crusher and via belts to the picking table; from there it traveled through another crusher, onto sizer screens, then into washers and dryers. Outside, metal-helmeted men drop the hopper doors on nos. 134594 and 47859 to clean the cars, then lock them securely and hook the empties on a cable that lowers them down to the tipple.

Around noon the hoppers are eased into position and the coal comes cascading out. Not just "coal," either, for there is no such generality to a miner. This is inch-and-a-quarter-minus Beacon coal (no lump measuring more than 1¼ inches), a coke-oven fuel ordered by EG&FA's Norfolk office. As such it becomes C&O Tide 470 – a label meaning a specific grade of coal under movement to a certain buyer and destined to cross the piers at Newport News. At 12:20 p.m. hoppers 134594 and 47859 are under load and being coasted down into the yard – a measure of the 6,200 tons of coal that Wharton No. 2 will load this June 2 into 105 cars during two shifts.

The trek begins

The USRA 2-6-6-2 with the majestic 12-wheel Vanderbilt tank goes on about her work, spotting empties and gathering loads until at 2:15 p.m., she departs from the mine. The skipper gathers up his bills, climbs onto the steel caboose, unwinds the handbrake, and lets it drift downgrade in the wake of the vanishing hoppers. This procedure permits the flagman to hop on and off, lining up the switches and derails in the Wharton No. 2 yard, without the necessity of continually stopping and starting a tonnage train on a grade. Down at the wye at Barrett, the hack joins its brood, the air is cut in, and Extra 1498 West proceeds to Wharton No. 1 to pick up more loads.

For the men aboard the caboose, the day that began with a nine o'clock call is almost done, and there's time to relax on the rear platform as the hoppers hold to the 30-mile-per-hour speed limit along the black waters of Pond Fork. The ties creak like new shoes, tie plates bounce on the bridges, and the flagman beeps the monkey-tail air whistle at the

insistence of miners' children. At each dusty grade crossing, a line of cars driven by helmeted men of the mines waits impatiently for the hoppers to clear. At 4:26, the extra is "dead" in Danville, safely tucked inside yard limits.

Within two hours, bobbing of electric lanterns and slamming of journal lids announce the approach of the car inspectors to the loaded hoppers. Their examination is brief but thorough. Skilled eyes roam over side bearing bolster, brake beam, brake hangers, brake shoes, and spring plank. Coupler, knuckle pin, and safety appliances such as ladders and steps are all checked. Next, the bane of the railroad – a hotbox – is thwarted as an inspector feels the journal, checks the brass and wedge, and makes sure, by a tug on his hook, that the oil-soaked waste isn't beginning to "grab." If needed, lubricant is added, then the inspectors proceed on down the dark and narrow canyons between the black, white-lettered cars.

At 9 p.m., the Danville switcher goes to work. At least they call her a "switcher," but she's actually a 2-6-6-2. Shuffling up loaded hoppers is no work for a six-coupled yard engine. All night long she labors to the accompaniment of thudding couplers and rumbling draft gear, and as dawn

Chesapeake & Ohio hopper 47859 is at left as the journey from tipple (Wharton No. 2) to tidewater begins deep in the West Virginia mountains (above). Inch-and-a-quarter-minus is dumped into the 47859, its mobile container for the 512 miles down to tidewater (below).

nears, the net result is a column of 135 loads with a caboose on one end and a 2-8-4 called for 5 a. m. on the other. This is Extra 2731 East, and not far from the tender are hoppers 134594 and 47859, their tanks and pipes inhaling as train-line air pressure builds up to the pace set by cross-compound pumps mounted on the Kanawha's pilot beam.

The mists hang heavy and chilly over Danville, but the calls

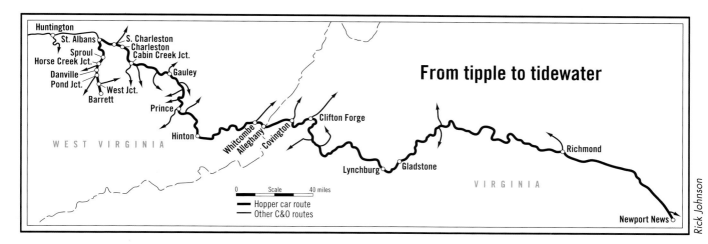

From tipple to tidewater

Scale
0   40 miles
▬▬ Hopper car route
— Other C&O routes

Rick Johnson

of bobwhites and crickets herald a new day – Friday, June 3 – when the 2-8-4 starts to pull at 6:40.

Key commodity for C&O

The loaded hoppers riding along behind the Kanawha are clicking off a splendid year for Chesapeake & Ohio. Coal tonnage is up one-third, and when the books are closed on 1955, the total will almost equal the record-breaking year of 1951. C&O is having its cake and eating it too. Aware of the vulnerability of a one-commodity carrier, even a coal road, Chessie began diversifying its traffic immediately after World War II. The absorption of Pere Marquette helped, as did more emphasis on car-ferry operations spanning Lake Michigan. Within 12 years, some 1,200 industries were persuaded to locate on-line, particularly in the Detroit area and in the chemical-atom empires mushrooming in the Ohio and Kanawha river valleys. Mileage-hungry merchandisers like *Speedwest* pounded past the familiar coal drags in their urgency to meet first- and second-morning delivery promises.

Coal? On C&O at least, the black giant had just been playing possum. After hitting a peak of 196 million dollars back in 1951, coal and coke revenues slid to 185 million in 1952, then 164 million in 1953, and finally lurched down to 138 million dollars in 1954. All the while, Chessie kept soliciting merchandise with one hand and

Hopper histories

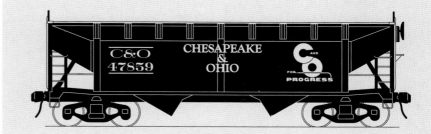

Car number: 47859

Birthplace and date: American Car & Foundry Company, Huntington, W. Va., 1946.

Dimensions: Length inside 33 feet; width inside 9 feet 6 inches; height from rail to top of sides 10 feet 5¼ inches; light weight 39,900 pounds.

Capacity: 50 tons

Repairs received to date: None other than usual light repair track attention.

Mileage: Individual car mileage records not kept but based upon averages; No. 47859 should have rolled 117,000 miles by the summer of 1955.

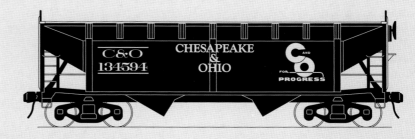

Car number: 134594

Birthplace and date: Pullman-Standard Car Manufacturing Company, Michigan City, Ind., December 1939.

Dimensions: Length inside 33 feet; width inside 9 feet 6 inches; height from rail to top of sides 10 feet 5¼ inches; light weight 40,300 pounds.

Capacity: 50 tons

Repairs received to date: In addition to usual light repair track attention, No. 134594 received program or heavy repairs once – in November 1951.

Mileage: An estimated 210,000 miles as of the summer of 1955.

9

W.A. Akin, Jr.

W.A. Akin, Jr.

How to prevent a hotbox (left): A Danville car inspector turns his hook around the journal to forestall a waste grab. Above, hoppers 47859 and 14594 are coupled up for the journey to the C&O main line and then on to Newport News.

grooming its vast coal-car fleet with the other. And in 1955, C&O was ready when the giant flexed his muscles, when national coal production climbed 19 percent. No one was less surprised than President Walter J. Tuohy. It takes a ton of coal to make a ton of steel, he says, and notes that the electric power industry – which now burns more than twice the coal mined on C&O – expects to double its capacity by 1965 and triple that by 1975. Western Europe needs coal, the atom industry needs coal, chemical plants need coal. No, Tuohy isn't surprised. And because of that, not a single mine on his railroad is missing a day's production in this booming 1955 because of a car shortage. Score one for faith and foresight.

Across the line
A train ahead of Extra 2731 making pickups and set-outs stabs the coal drag a couple of times, but before the sun reaches its meridian, the 2-8-4 brings her hoppers off the Coal River Subdivision and onto the main line at St. Albans, takes on a tank of water, and takes off eastward on multiple track up the Kanawha River Valley. By 12:29 p.m., the coal is into Handley, W.Va., and a diesel yard engine is cutting off the caboose and rear 20 or so cars to squeeze the train into the yard.

Standing cars earn no money, so Handley operates as a relay station instead of a storage site. A crew is called at 1:15 to move coal that has barely stopped rolling. There is just time to nail a cut of manifest cars on the head end (for the Virginian interchange at Deepwater), then an A-B-A diesel combo composed of three dusty blue and yellow F7 units takes over for the next 72½ miles to Hinton. In that distance, the elevation rises from 631 to 1,382 feet, but the grade stays below half a percent all the way as the rails follow first the Kanawha River, then one of its tributaries – the New River. Rambling along in the echo of chanting V16s, hoppers 134594 and 47859 swing past Gauley Bridge, W.Va., then into New River Gorge – 60 miles of canyon in which the heartbeats of the yelling diesels bounce off walls that rise to an altitude of 1,300 feet. Hawk's Nest, Horseshoe Bend, Sandstone Falls . . . the 145 loads go trundling along obediently behind the diesel master as coal goes to market as Tide 470 is beckoned toward the piers of Newport News. As the sun abdicates its crown and shadows deepen, the coal slips inside yard limits at Hinton, W.Va., foot of the climb across the Alleghenies.

There's work to be done in Hinton: Tonnage must be adjusted out of regard for the mountain

ahead and the helper power available; coal in demand like Tide 470 must be placed on a first-out basis; there are gondolas loaded with Army float bridges tabbed for the first drag east; power and crews must be called; and the dispatcher must find a vacant slot on his train sheet so that the coal doesn't stab a passenger train or a merchandiser as it's laboriously hoisted to the summit of the Alleghenies.

The engine crew gets a 10:45 p.m. call, and not long after that its three-unit, 4,500-horsepower F7 is idling back to lock couplers with 100 cars – more than 8,200 tons of inertia. "Covered tops," the engineer calls his regulation cab units out of affection for the more popular road-switcher models, but the horsepower is equal, and tonight every pound of tractive effort will be needed because the usual helper is absent.

At 11:32 p.m., the five-tone air chime talks up, and the throttle comes back on a calculated risk. Within less than 1½ hours, No. 2, the *George Washington*, will be climbing the mountain. The question is written across the railroaders' Hamiltons: Can 4,500 horses lift 8,200 tons 50 miles up a .57-percent ruling grade and be in the clear at Alleghany for No. 2?

The V16s wind up and the generators try for a tenor note, then settle for soprano. The wheel-slip light flashes in the darkened cab, sand coaxes 24 driving wheels, and – with the needle laying hard on 1,400 amperes – Extra 7089 East comes alive. Midnight and June 4 is born as the diesels go grinding upgrade with the moon-illuminated Greenbrier River down below on one side and a cliff of slide-detector-fenced rock on the other. Little Bend Tunnel … Big Bend Tunnel … 11 miles per hour and 900 amps … 18 miles per hour and 800 amps … finally 30 as the diesels pay close attention to a hogger who believes in putting 'em in the last notch and leaving 'em there.

Harts Run at 11 miles per hour and 900 amperes as the grade bares its teeth at .57 percent uncompensated, and a while later the diesels threaten to disturb the sleep behind the regal white columns of White Sulphur Springs. Up … and up … and on up – and then, minutes before 2 a.m., Extra 7089 is leaving the main and taking siding at Alleghany, 2,072 feet above sea level. From the west, a rotating headlight and a snarl of E8s and No. 2 – all blue and yellow and roller bearing – goes gliding by on time. A sharp dispatcher and a talented engineer have pulled off a sample of smart railroading on the mountain – and Tide 470 is that much nearer to the sea.

Retainers are set up, and at 2:17, the coal begins moving down the 1.14 percent of the eastern slope as sand, dynamic braking, air, and hot brake shoes work in unison to hold 8,200 tons to the legal limit of 20 miles per hour. The Hamilton numerals read 4:07 when the coal is "dead" in Clifton Forge.

Final leg

Once again, the coal must be classified, and by 8 a.m. hoppers 134594 and 47894 are coming across the crest of the Clifton Forge hump. Some 18 riders are at work easing the hoppers down into the classification tracks;

Chesapeake & Ohio Mallet (2-6-6-2) 1498 kicks off the air and ambles off downgrade to Barrett with loads; the caboose at left will follow "light."

retarders aren't practical because to accommodate them the east end of the yard would have to be raised 16 feet, so great is the difference in elevation, and as yet the economics just don't justify that expenditure.

Gradually the tide coal builds up into two blocks on tracks 4 and 5, and soon a pair of GP7 road-switchers is nosing forth from the engine terminal to assemble the hoppers into a single 160-car, 14,000-ton train. Actually, 160 cars is not the limit of the Geeps' capacity down the gently descending James River Line to Richmond; it's just a convenient, flexible limit in view of such considerations as starting and stopping and siding lengths. The line, which knifes through the Blue Ridge Mountain range on a river-grade profile, is one of those natural boons out of which 68.1-percent operating ratios (C&O's in 1955) are made. Consider the plight of Norfolk & Western, for example, which

encounters a 1.2-percent helper grade when lifting its coal across the same mountain.

At 11 a.m., the Geeps dig in (or rather, kick off the air in the descending yard at Clifton Forge), and within a handful of minutes tide coal is rolling at 40 miles per hour. Five men and 3,000 horse-power taking a net payload of 11,200 tons of coal to market at 40 miles per hour – keep that firmly in mind because it's a speed-tonnage performance no other medium of transport can match, particularly in cost. Flexible transport, made up of 50-ton and 70-ton units . . . all-weather transport, too . . . and regulated, self-supporting, tax-paying transport as well.

The coal reaches the division town of Gladstone, Va., at 3:09 p.m., is reshuffled, and leaves behind the same Geeps at 7:19 and reaches Fulton Yard in Richmond at 11:30. Tide 470 is hot now because a ship slated to load it is due at the Newport News

One of the C&O's thoroughbred 2-8-4s waits impatiently to return to the main line with loads of tidewater-bound bituminous.

piers at Sunday midnight. As of this Saturday night, 24 hours from deadline, the railroad is calling in 470 – two hoppers of it in Newport News, 118 more in Richmond (including the 134594 and 37859), 52 in Gladstone, and 50 located in Clifton Forge. Enter the art of railroading again. Newport News handles 240 different classifications of coal and between 40 and 50 grades of it. Ordering and receiving the correct number of cars of the requested classification and at the appointed time – that's the ticket.

Tide 470 is hot: The sharp bark of the Alco yard engine kicking hoppers about outside Fulton's yard office means as much. In the yellow glare of overhead yard lights, another 160-car train is assembled and power is coordinated: the two tireless Geeps that came from Clifton Gorge on the head end plus two more GP7s cut in ahead of the caboose to boost the 14,000 tons up the 4 miles of .63 percent immediately east of

Fulton Yard. At 3:17 a.m., June 5, 1955, 6,000 horsepower worth of Geeps (plus an initial kick by a 1,000-horsepower yard engine) lean into the awful effort of starting big tonnage on a grade. Traction motors warm, sand is gobbled up by fitful drivers – finally inertia loses out as 160 cars move out and up from Fulton Yard.

The speedometers of the Geeps show 8 miles per hour, and the output goes to 1,000 amperes. A slumbering Richmond slips behind as 64 cylinders go yelling through the night to keep an appointment at tidewater. A pause at the summit to unleash the helpers, then the Geeps ahead have a reasonably easy time of it down the Peninsula Subdivision and into the receiving yard at Newport News. The sun is up as the Geeps come snaking their load through the standing lines of loaded hoppers – 7,627 of them in one yard – and coast to a halt at 6:29 a.m.

Tide 470 nears its final destination on railroad property as the Mystic Steamship Company's

Arlington is docked at midnight, and at 12:10 a.m. hoppers 134594 and 47859 roll out of the darkness, across the scales, and into the grip of the iron mule whose steel fist shoves them up into the car dumper. Upside down now, and inch-and-a-quarter-minus Beacon coal dug in West Virginia Thursday morning pours onto the belts and is funneled into the *Arlington's* holds minutes after midnight Sunday.

To be specific: No. 134594 unloads 121,700 pounds of coal while 47859 gives up 122,000 pounds. The charge for these 121 short tons from Wharton No. 2 to Newport News – 5612 miles – comes to $3.66 per ton or 7.48 cents per ton-mile, plus 4.5 cents per ton for dumping at tidewater.

Numbers 134594 and 47859 race vainly up the kickback, falter, then coast back past the dumper into the blackness of the yard. So much for 243,700 pounds of the 61.6 million tons of coal originated by C&O in 1955.

Where's the coal?

Norfolk & Western

I f we're going to model railroads that earn a significant part of their keep by hauling coal, it helps to know where that coal comes from and a little bit about how it got there in the first place. The map of North American coal reserves (**fig. 1**) shows four major fields of anthracite (hard) coal in northeastern Pennsylvania – and almost nowhere else! Skip a hundred miles or so to the west and you encounter the vast bituminous (soft) coalfields of western Pennsylvania on down through Maryland and the Virginias into northern Alabama. What happened to the coal in between? And why are some coal seams (not *veins*; that term applies to ore) literally as hard as a rock, while other beds are much softer or even brown, with signs of vegetation still evident?

The rock that burns is found under a considerable portion of the U.S. and parts of Canada and Mexico. Here a high grade of bituminous coal in a mine served by the Norfolk & Western in southern West Virginia is being mined and loaded onto a conveyor by mechanical means, as opposed to the picks and shovels used by this miner's predecessors.

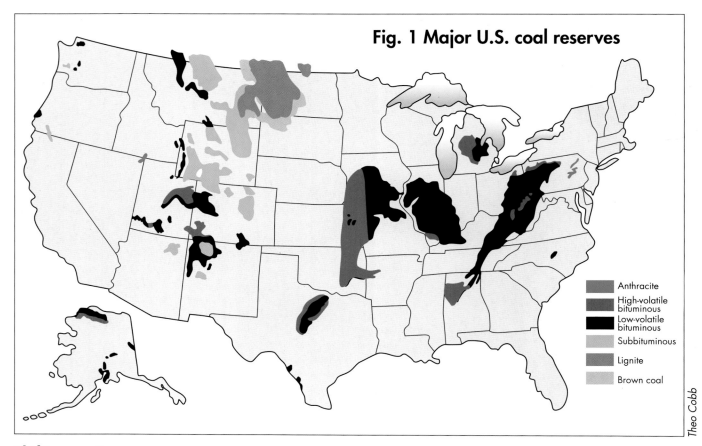

Fig. 1 Major U.S. coal reserves

Anthracite
High-volatile bituminous
Low-volatile bituminous
Subbituminous
Lignite
Brown coal

Theo Cobb

Shifting continents

As any recent geology textbook will show, North America was once part of a vast gathering of continents called Pangaea. Several hundred million years ago, the major landmasses were not only butted close together, but located farther to the south. What split off to become North America then straddled the equator – magnetic evidence frozen into the rocks suggests it was turned sideways so the equator ran north-south through the center of the continent – where lush tropical rain forests flourished in a carbon dioxide-rich atmosphere.

Later, as the future continents jostled one another for position before inching apart on tectonic plates, the central part of the continent subsided, allowing a tropical ocean to occupy the areas where today we grow equally vast acres of corn and wheat and soybeans. Coastal mountain chains were elevated like a car's hood folding up in a front-end

North American coal is found from the Canadian Maritime Provinces on south through the Appalachians into Mexico, and in the West along the Rockies into Canada and in parts of Alaska. Almost 30 percent of the world's coal reserves lie in North America; China and the former Soviet states also have major coal reserves. Although coal production declined after oil and gas supplanted coal for home heating, its use for electric power generation has caused a tremendous upswing in rail ton-miles since the 1970s. In 1979, there were about 6,000 coal mines in 26 states, with 40 percent mined underground, the latter mostly east of the Mississippi.

collision. As the mountains eroded, the adjacent rain forests were buried beneath mud and sand. More tropical forests grew and again were buried. The weight of thousands of feet of overburden compressed the plants like a vise. What we know today as coal was born.

The "new" Appalachians

The Appalachians where we find coal deposits today are not the original mountains. The ancient Appalachians were shoved higher than today's Rockies more than 400 million years ago, then eroded away. The coal-to-be forests flourished in the Carboniferous Era about 300 million years ago. A second orogeny (mountain-

building episode) occurred about 200 million years ago, when today's Appalachians were shoved skyward. If you stand atop one of today's Appalachian peaks, you can see that their summits have similar heights. This marks the former peneplain that was re-elevated to form today's Appalachians.

This is an important characteristic for modelers of Appalachian railroading to observe: The summits of the mountain ridges should all be within a narrow range of elevations to denote the surface of this between-orogenies plain.

As the second batch of Appalachians eroded, seams of coal that had been uplifted with the other

Tony Koester

Coal overtook wood as a source of heat in the late 1890s, and the center of coal production until relatively recent times was in the central Appalachians. Among the major coal roads was the pioneering Baltimore & Ohio, which had a major coal marshalling yard at Keyser, W. Va. (also see page 4). Following the merger of the B&O, Chesapeake & Ohio, and Western Maryland to form the Chessie System in 1973, locomotive consists were colorful and varied, as is evident in this June 1976 photo (above). Earlier that day, Baltimore & Ohio 7599 in its pre-Chessie System livery works serpentine Keyser Yard before the summertime mountain haze had burned off (below).

Tony Koester

sedimentary rocks were exposed (**fig. 2**). In what became northeastern Pennsylvania, the coal beds were folded and compressed into anthracite (hard) coal (**fig. 3**). The mud that covered them was compressed into shale and often metamorphosed into slate. West of the Ridge and Valley Province, the coal had been elevated but not folded. The mud and sand that covered them became shale and sandstone. Limestone, the lithified remnants of seashells that rained down to the tropical ocean's floor, may also be found above and below coal seams.

Elsewhere on the continent, similar processes deposited lush, thick beds of vegetation that were buried and turned into peat, then lignite, and in many cases bituminous coal. The folding that took place along the spine of the Appalachians did not affect the Central and Western coal beds, so with rare exceptions hard coal is confined to northeastern

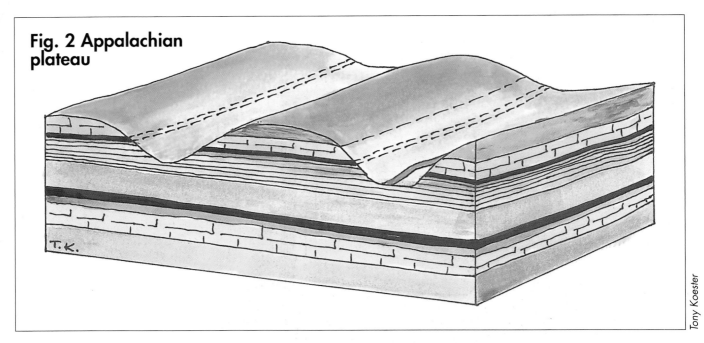

Fig. 2 Appalachian plateau

T.K.

Tony Koester

West of the Ridge and Valley Province, which runs through eastern Pennsylvania and eastern West Virginia, the Appalachian Plateau was elevated without being severely folded, and bituminous coal beds (dark layers) were exposed as creeks and rivers relentlessly cut down toward sea level (fig. 2). Along the eastern edge of the Appalachians, however, the horizontal sedimentary beds of coal and rock were folded and faulted, converting bituminous coal to anthracite and creating extremely difficult mining conditions (fig. 3).

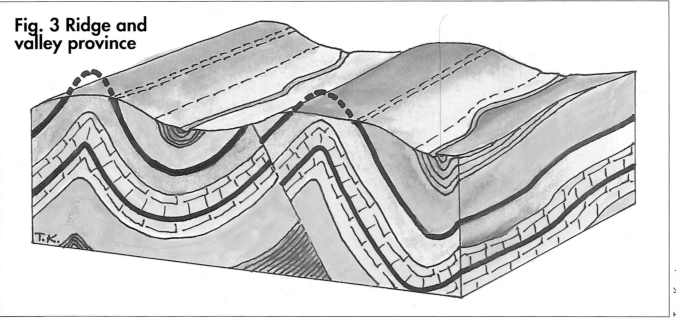

Fig. 3 Ridge and valley province

T.K.

Tony Koester

Pennsylvania. The exceptions are where volcanic rock penetrated the soft-coal beds, cooking out the volatiles with heat rather than eons of unyielding pressure. Without the undulated anticlines, synclines, and faults typical of Pennsylvania's anthracite beds, Midwestern, Western, Canadian, and Mexican coal beds are much flatter and therefore easier to mine. Conversely, Midwestern coal beds lie underground, as there are no outcroppings on the sides of mountains to allow drift mining.

Digging coal

Coal was discovered in North America not long after the early European settlers shifted from a bare subsistence level into an exploratory, resource-development mode. One might suspect that coal's properties as a fuel were discovered when someone lined his campfire with these black rocks, only to have them add to the conflagration, but coal was already known on the other side of the Atlantic.

Coal was almost handed to these pioneers on a platter. All they had to do was to venture into the mountains and look up. Seams of coal, some tens of feet thick, were exposed and ready for the taking. Miners merely hacked out an opening into the coal seam and followed it back into the hills. Mines utilizing such horizontal entryways are called drift mines (**fig. 4**), and are commonly found in southern Appalachia. To provide for drainage, entryways into level drift mines are cut at a slight angle.

Where the coal lies deep underground, as in the northern Appalachians and Midwest, either gently sloping entryways are cut into the native rock (**fig. 5**), or vertical shafts are excavated (**fig. 6**). Slope mines are employed where the coal seam dips at a shallow angle, allowing the entryway to simply follow the slope of the seam.

Miners originally left pillars of coal to support the ceiling or roof of the main as they drilled and blasted out the coal. Short- and long-wall mining machines allow more of the coal to be removed, as the ceiling is allowed to collapse as the mining machine withdraws. In more recent times, enormous electric shovels can economically strip away tens or even hundreds of feet of the overburden above important coal seams, allowing pillars to be reclaimed or new seams to be mined, as shown in the photos on page 18.

First stop: the Appalachians
Now that we've reviewed how coal was formed, where the various types of coal are, and how it's mined, let's begin our overview of the coal industry and the railroads that served it.

Fig. 4 Drift mine

Fig. 5 Slope mine

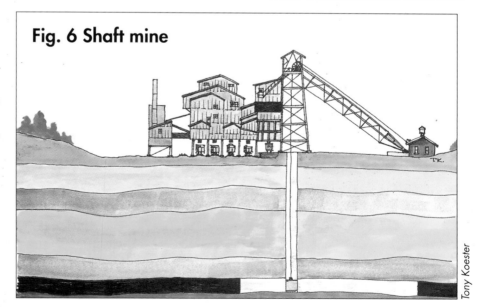

Fig. 6 Shaft mine

Figures 4, 5, and 6 show the three basic configurations of coal mines. At top is a *drift mine*, where the entryway follows a coal seam horizontally into an exposed mountainside. A *slope mine* (middle) may follow a dipping coal seam or may be an access tunnel cut at a shallow angle to allow loaded coal cars to be pulled up the incline. A *shaft mine* (bottom) heads vertically underground to tap deep coal seams.

Open-pit or surface mining (formerly called strip mining) requires large shovels and other heavy-duty earth-moving equipment. The huge shovel above works a mine on the Craig Branch of the Rio Grande in August 1977. As a safety engineer, photographer John Roberts has inspected many underground and surface mining operations, including the one shown below where a lot of overburden has been stripped away to get to a coal seam.

Kenneth E. Kurtz, John Roberts collection

Peach Creek Yard at Logan, W.Va. (above), was an important coal-marshalling point on the Chesapeake & Ohio. The well-worn sedimentary rock above the GP38 is horizontal, a hallmark of the Appalachian Plateau. Water helped cover the tropical forests that became coal seams, and it then cut paths through the mountains to expose those same beds, so coal mining and railroading in the mountains are closely aligned with major streams. The prep plant below served the C&O's West Fork Subdivision at Van, W.Va., in 1988.

John Roberts

Richard J. Cook

THREE

Tams, W.Va., named for a coal baron, was served by the Chesapeake & Ohio (to the rear) and Virginian. In June 1950, the community and its school looked far better than most of the region's coal camps, such as the one shown on page 21. Here two of the C&O's ubiquitous 2-6-6-2s work at the north end of town.

"I owe my soul to the company store" was the refrain in Tennessee Ernie Ford's popular 1950s singing lament about the working conditions faced by Appalachian coal miners. This was especially true in the southern Appalachian coalfields, where coal barons built entire towns for the miners. The owners were fiercely independent and paternalistic, making it clear to all concerned that what was good for the company was good for the town and people who lived and worked there. Miners were initially paid in scrip or given credit at the company store, which provided all of the basic necessities – but at a price somewhat higher than independent stores in the region. There was no way to save U.S. dollars to spend elsewhere, so the practice was finally outlawed, but coal operators continued to ban commercial stores or private homes on land they owned or leased, which was most of it.

Creating a whole new world

The anthracite coalfields of northeastern Pennsylvania and the northern bituminous fields in Appalachia were located in areas that already had been developed to some extent. Company towns, called *mine patches* in hard-coal country and *coal camps* in the soft-coal fields, were erected as needed, but many miners lived in private homes on land not owned or leased by the coal companies.

The southern Appalachian fields grew in tune to the progress of the railroads, mainly the Chesapeake & Ohio and the Norfolk & Western, and later the Virginian. These lines were pushed back into wilderness, and everything from the tipples to the town – and even the miners – had to be imported. Some mines employed local mountain men, but they were as independent as the capitalists who owned the mines, quitting work when they had accumulated enough money to get by for the next several months, just as they had done on their farms. Mine owners viewed

The houses in this coal camp were in dire need of paint in March 1975. With a few notable exceptions, coal camps in the southern Appalachian soft-coal fields were often ramshackle affairs offering no more than a bare-bones level of comfort.

this as a lack of work ethic and hired recruiters to find men overseas who didn't see "vacations" as an entitlement.

No matter one's race or nationality, however, coal mining was – and still is – a tough and dangerous way to earn a living.

The company town

Since many company towns were so isolated, all of the basic needs had to be provided on site via the company store. This included a place to buy clothing, furniture, and groceries, along with a post office and barbershop.

The harsh realities of mining, coupled with low wages, especially in the non-unionized southern Appalachian coal fields, caused miners to head north looking for better wages in other mines, steel mills, and auto plants.

Therefore, some company towns – notably Holden and Widen in West Virginia and

Jenkins and Lynch in eastern Kentucky – were built as model communities. Amenities such as homes with plastered walls and ceilings, paved streets, parks, sewer systems, running water, garbage pick-up, a dairy, a swimming pool, theater, community center with library, and even an ice cream parlor and saloon were incorporated in an effort to retain the miners. Even so, there's no mistaking the geometric monotony of a coal patch, as the accompanying photos from various eras clearly indicate.

The days when coal companies directly owned entire towns are gone, but things haven't changed much in some areas. During a 1970s visit to a former company town, I asked whether a family I met owned their home. "Oh, no, we rent it." From the local coal company, Island Creek Coal? "No, that's not legal anymore. We rent it from Island Creek Realty Company."

Tony Koester

Tony Koester

The days of austere uniformity in company towns, known as coal camps when they were located up an isolated "holler," were clearly gone by the time of these 1974 views along the Clinchfield RR in and near Dante ("dant"), Va. Company homes often provided front-row seats to railroading, and even Dante's steepled church abutted the CRR main. Dante's small engine terminal, yard, and scales were located just beyond the church.

Tony Koester

This former company town near Rum Junction, W.Va., on the Chesapeake & Ohio was clearly a cut above the town shown on page 21, but these homes were leased rather than owned and still wore "company colors" when photographed in July 1975. "Air conditioning" was confined to sitting out on the front porch on sultry summer days. The constant presence of an active railroad spur in the front yard was a fact of life, and children quickly learned how to stay out of harm's way. Local entertainment was sparse, but a boy can always find a way to enjoy a small stream.

Tony Koester

A pair of Virginian Train Masters runs long-hood forward, as usual, above Slab Fork, W.Va., with eastbound manifest freight no. 72 headed for Roanoke, Va. (above). A spur to a large prep plant and coal mine heads off to the right behind the depot. By the time the author visited Slab Fork in October 1998 (left), the coal facilities and depot were gone, but many of the company houses were still in use.

Company houses ranged from uninsulated one-story cabins with board-and-batten siding to two-story homes with most of the basic amenities including, in modern times, a tree-shaded yard without tracks running through it. These photos were taken in 1975, but except for the vehicles, the scenes depicted in the two lower photos could date back to Depression years.

Tony Koester

The author kitbashed a row of company houses for North Durbin, W.Va. (above), on his Allegheny Midland HO model railroad using the popular Ma's Place/Speedy Andrew's Repair Shop kit offered by several importers (below). New tar-paper-covered roofs and porches were fabricated. Here one of the Midland Road's I-class compound 2-6-6-2s rolls through town using trackage rights over the Western Maryland between North Durbin and Glady.

Dave Frary

The town of Coal Fork (page 27, top) on the author's AM represents a commercial settlement not under the thumb of the local coal operator, so independent stores lined the main drag, such as it was. Just outside of town, however, were company homes, which the author kitbashed from Rix one-story house kits. The company houses at Low Gap (page 27, bottom) are Grandt Line Silverton homes with the roof pitch decreased to 30 degrees; the company store is made from two Smalltown U.S.A. hardware store kits on a raised foundation. Many kits for company houses are now available, and company stores are easy to kitbash. Compare the shapes of the prototypes shown on pages 28 and 29 to store and factory kits to find suitable candidates such as Campbell's Shrock's Meat Pkg., American Model Builders' Ellington's Mercantile, and several Design Preservation Model stores.

Tony Koester

Tony Koester

There's no mistaking this structure at Yolyn, W.Va., on a Chesapeake & Ohio branch as anything but a company store. Jim Boyd photographed it with Alco RSD-12s alongside when it was painted gray; it later got a coat of pale yellow paint. Plans of the prototype and of John Roberts' selectively compressed model appeared in the April 1983 *Railroad Model Craftsman*; a resin kit of the latter is offered by Funaro and Camerlingo.

Jim Boyd

Mike Brestel

The New River Company's Oakwood company store was a substantial brick affair that sat near a yard at Carlisle, W.Va., where the Virginian and C&O swapped loaded hoppers.

Tony Koester

Occasionally, company stores were located adjacent to the mines and preparation plants, a consequence of having to cram everything into the narrow valleys cut by streams. Note the ubiquitous raised front porch.

Tony Koester

These buildings appear to be the old wood and more-recent block company stores near Rum Junction on the C&O, although the wood building may have been a rooming house.

Tony Koester

This wood company store is located near the Clinchfield at Trammel, Va.

Tony Koester

This classic wooden tribute to the coal-baron era stands at Burnwell, W.Va., on C&O's Imperial Subdivision.

John Roberts

Especially in the northern bituminous and anthracite fields, there has long been a strong union presence, and a United Mine Workers union hall such as this one is a signature structure in coal country.

John Roberts

Ron Piskor

FOUR

Quinnimont, W.Va., is located deep in the New River gorge where the Laurel Subdivision leaves the Chesapeake & Ohio main. The depot and a water tank were located within the wye, but the area became famous for "QN Cabin," a yardmaster's office with a tower atop. This photo shows how it looked in 1972.

Late in the 20th century, before the center of coal production moved west to the Powder River Basin coalfields around Gillette, Wyo., central Appalachia was the country's main coal-producing region. In 1946, for example, West Virginia ranked first in coal production, followed by Pennsylvania. Back in 1929, 91 percent of coal production was east of the Mississippi. In this chapter, we'll discuss railroading in the Appalachian bituminous fields; Chapter 5 will look at anthracite roads.

Railroads serving the mines that tapped into the widespread bituminous beds of the central Appalachians included the Baltimore & Ohio, Chesapeake & Ohio, Clinchfield, Louisville & Nashville, and Western Maryland (all now CSX); New York Central and Pennsylvania (Conrail, then split between CSX and Norfolk Southern); and the Norfolk & Western,

Southern, and Virginian (part of NS today).

Some of the world's most-potent steam locomotives – the Lima-built 2-6-6-6 Alleghenies of the C&O, the near-twin Blue Ridges of the VGN, and the Y6b 2-8-8-2s of the N&W – were employed in coal service. Smaller compound Mallets typically worked the mine branches.

Changing times

The end of the 1950s saw the demise of the demand for steam coal as diesels vanquished the last of the once-enormous steam fleet. Beefy six-motor diesels from Alco, Electro-Motive, and General Electric were clawing their way over the ridges with carloads of coal (see Chapter 9), but these locomotives no longer burned what they hauled.

By the late 1960s, the demand for coal to heat homes had also largely disappeared, although I recall seeing trucks delivering coal to eastern Pennsylvania homes in the latter part of the 20th century.

These individual customers were replaced by the growing demands for electric power as well as by customers overseas. The solitary hopper headed for the local coal yard thus became as rare as a steam locomotive, and unit trains billed to a single large customer became the norm, as we'll discuss in Chapter 8.

Appalachian highlights

The following pages include vignettes of coal and railroad operations. Such images inspired me to spend a quarter of a century building and operating an HO coal road in my basement, and I hope they enhance your modeling as well.

Maps of the C&O in the West Virginia coalfields appeared in the December 2001 *Trains*, and of L&N coal mines in the August 2005 issue. Soft-coal mines open to the public include the Beckley Exhibition Mine in Beckley, W.Va. (www.beckleymine.com), and the Seldom Seen Mine in Punxsutawney, Pa.

The author visited QN in 1973 (top) and eventually built an HO model of the structure from scratch (above) for his Allegheny Midland layout.

Russell H. Heffley

This vintage print shows the substantial machine shops and boiler plant associated with the Eureka No. 35 mine owned by Berwind Coal Co. in Pennsylvania. Berwind hoppers are available in HO from Bowser.

Tony Koester

Tony Koester

Muskingham Electric used modern GE electric locomotives to haul coal from the mine head directly to a power plant in southeastern Ohio. Note the horizontal strata typical of sedimentary rock in the Appalachian Plateau.

Muskingham Electric used a small GE switcher to move cars at the mine loader. Both ME photos were taken in February 1974.

A pair of Monongahela GEs lead a coal train at Bailey Mine near Waynesburg, Pa., in April 1991 (above). Years earlier, the railroad gained fame for placing former New York Central Baldwin Sharks into service (see Chapter 9).

One of the largest coal preparation plants in southeastern Ohio was on the Adena, Cadiz & New Athens Ry. (below), switched by the Wheeling & Lake Erie (later Nickel Plate, then Norfolk & Western) near Georgetown. The mix of road names on the hoppers evident in 1976 attests to the lines that merged into the N&W.

Courtesy C&O Historical Society

The Republic Steel Co.'s tipple at Republic, Ky., had only two load-out tracks, as a full range of prepared coal sizes wasn't needed for steel production. The author kitbashed a model of this tipple (below right) using Walthers New River Coal kits, as described in October 1998 *Model Railroader*.

Courtesy C&O Historical Society

Tony Koester

The Dixie Mining Co. truck dump on the Chesapeake & Ohio at Pikesville, Ky., was a classic two-track tipple incorporating a truck scale and rudimentary coal cleaning and crushing facilities. Coal was trucked in from a nearby strip or surface mine. The three photos above show the operation in 1974 and 1975 before the tracks were relocated.

The Kelly (left) and Wharton (right) prep plants on the C&O below Danville, W.Va., are typical of relatively modern (for the late steam era) plants in central and southern Appalachia. The branch bypasses the tipple to reach additional mines farther up the line. Empty hoppers are spotted uphill from the mine, then fed as needed through the tipple using gravity, a winch, or a dedicated switch engine.

Trammel, Va., on the Clinchfield featured this imposing truck dump that loaded out a pair of tracks, one under the tipple and one between the tipple and the CRR main line. A smaller pair of truck dumps was visible when the author visited the area in October 1975. He then kitbashed a similar three-track version in HO, using Walthers New River Coal kit components, for the Coal Fork Subdivision of his Allegheny Midland. The project appeared in the October 1998 *Model Railroader*. The Clinchfield – formally the Carolina, Clinchfield & Ohio – ran from Spartanburg, S. C., north to an end-to-end connection with the Chesapeake & Ohio at Elkhorn City, Ky., along the way traversing some of the most spectacular country in the East, if not the entire continent. Today the two lines form a seamless part of CSX, but coal is still king.

Tony Koester

Tony Koester

Berta, Va. (above), marked the junction of the Clinchfield-operated Haysi RR with the CRR main line. In 1975, the Atomic Fuel Co. had a truck dump located on a ridge above a tunnel that fed a single spur. Empties were spotted between the turnout and the conveyor, then pulled under the loader using a winch.

In April 1973, the Haysi's single F7 B unit (below) was being used to move cars around a tipple on the branch.

Tony Koester

The cross-track loader in the background was fed by a modern prep plant located high on the hill to the right (west) of the Clinchfield main line at Roaring Fork, Va. Coal was trucked into the loader at the left.

Tony Koester

The energy crisis of the early 1970s ended the doldrums of the Appalachian coalfields and created car and motive-power shortages. The Louisville & Nashville supplemented its already sizable Alco fleet of RS-3s and Alco Centuries with additional ex-Seaboard Coast Line C-420s plus those acquired in the Tennessee Central and Monon mergers. A pair of C-420s worked a new tipple by a general store near Olvah, Ky. (above). Big-brother C-630 1429 and two GEs power a coal train toward Patio (Winchester), Ky. (below left), and (below right) a big GE pauses at a signal near Pineville, Ky., also in the spring of 1974.

One of the most-accomplished modelers of 1970s southern Appalachian coal railroading is John Wilkes of Winter Haven, Fla., as these three photos clearly attest. A Louisville & Nashville Alco RS-3 (top) works the Joyce Ann No. 3 prep plant, which is fed by the truck dump at left. Another RS-3 is dwarfed by the prep plant (center), where coal is cleaned and sized to customer specifications. The photo at the bottom of this page shows two Alco Century 420s that have a good roll on their charges as they swing past the Clospint tipple. John is now building a new and improved version of his HO railroad designed to support operation as authentic as his scenery and structures.

Paul Dolkos

Paul Dolkos

Paul Dolkos

The Virginian was one of two eastern coal haulers that made extensive use of electrification to move coal out of West Virginia to tidewater. At top, a trio of squareheads eases down a 1.3-percent grade at Oakdale, W.Va., on Sept. 4, 1953; note the classic Virginian Hotel and Texaco signs. Mullens (left) was the hub of the Virginian and the west end of the electrification; when the author photographed the motor barn in 1973, second-generation Norfolk & Western EMDs handled the road jobs. Virginian H24-66 Fairbanks-Morse Train Masters, the giants of the first-generation diesel era, had lost their yellow-and-black livery and were confined to switching the yard east of Mullens at Elmore by 1975 (below). Crews could afford to be welcoming back then, and Jim Boyd and the author were soon invited up into the cab.

Bluefield, which straddles the West Virginia-Virginia state line, was and remains a citadel on the Norfolk & Western (Norfolk Southern today). In May 1975, an SD45, running in typical long-hood-forward fashion, eases an eastbound coal drag into the yard past a series of buildings perfectly arranged as "background flats" (left). Space is at a premium in the mountains, so the porches on several buildings at Davey, W.Va., near the N&W main line (above) were simply extended out over a stream. A lone boxcar, almost a stranger in coal country, joins hoppers at a relatively modern coal tipple (bottom). It brought in mining supplies, perhaps bags of rock dust used to coat the walls (ribs) of the coal seams to help control methane gas emissions. As a result, mine passageways were not coal black, as one might expect, but instead were white!

Tony Koester

Tony Koester

The Western Maryland was a classy operation from the days when a fireball paint scheme adorned its steam and early diesel fleet. In the mid-1950s, the speed-lettering livery came into vogue, and was being replaced with the black-red-white "circus" scheme when the WM joined the Chessie System in 1973. At top, a mixed bag of the middle and last schemes on F units works on the Elkins line in May 1973. Lumber products were also a major reason for the WM's existence, and it was a major carrier of wood chips to the Westvaco paper mill at Luke, Md. This small chipping operation (left) was located at Slatyfork (Laurel Bank), W. Va. Chips are relatively light, so the WM extended the sides on some old coal hoppers. Chip cars were blocked at the head-end of the local out of Elkins (below) so the "whiffle dust" from coal hoppers wouldn't contaminate the chips. Note mid-train helpers; up to 11 big 2-8-0s were previously used to move coal up this grade!

Tony Koester

The Pennsy, and subsequently the Penn Central, was a major player in the bituminous coal market. Pennsy branches blanketed western Pennsylvania, and the railroad used big power such as class-I1 2-10-0s and, later, Alco Centuries to move the tonnage. Here a trio of Alco C-630s lugs a train through Warrenton, Ohio, in August 1972.

Chuck Yungkurth

Tony Koester

The Kelley's Creek & Northwestern used General Electric 70-ton diesels to move coal from minehead to river barges near Charleston, W. Va. This scene is in January 1970.

Miners are a resourceful lot, and this March 1976 view shows how old hopper car bodies were often employed in tipples as temporary storage bins for trucked-in coal.

Tony Koester

John Roberts

Tony Koester

Plant fertilizer (ammonium nitrate) mixed with diesel fuel creates an explosive used in mines. The photo at left shows a covered hopper car in front of an ammonium-nitrate unloader near Beckley, W. Va., in September 1987. At right, the author used a small cement-silo kit to serve this purpose at Gap Run, Va., on his HO scale Allegheny Midland layout.

Paul Dolkos

The Southern Railway also tapped into Appalachian bituminous coalfields, notably in the western tip of Virginia. Two F units lead a train on the former Interstate RR near Osaka, Va., in April 1968. Note the two extended-height twin hoppers.

David Baer; John Roberts collection

John Roberts

Many larger coal mines employed narrow-gauge railroads to move coal not only out of the mine but also a mile or more to the prep plant. A narrow-gauge mine lokey (above left) pulls a string of cars at Shanipin Mining Co. in Bobtown, Pa., in June 1989. In the photo above, a mine trip enters Lightfoot No. 1 mine behind an electric motor.

Tony Koester

Plenty of ventilation is the key to safe mining, so huge exhaust fans are found on the surface above the underground workings (left).

Jeff Kraker is an Interstate RR fan, so he based the design of the scratchbuilt Wise Coal Co.'s tipple at Derby, Va., on his freelanced HO Roanoke & Southern RR on the IRR's tipple at Dunbar. The tipple was flopped to allow coal to come in on the opposite side. The coke ovens, cast from masters Jeff made, are slightly compressed versions of those at Pine Branch on the Interstate.

Mike Rose and the author both used Con-Cor's HO Tucson Silver Mine kit as the basis for a small tipple. Mike's single-track Brockway Mine (left) is fed by a conveyor reaching up to a drift mine on the slope; the author's double-track version (right) is fed by a dump truck.

The colorful Ponfeigh tipple on the Baltimore & Ohio at Rockwood in Somerset County, Pa., was quite active in December 1967. The plant's compact size and track arrangement make it an ideal candidate for modeling.

King Coal Company

Bob Sobol

One of the most spectacular examples of Appalachian coal railroading in miniature was David Stewart's freelanced Appalachian & Ohio. This scene is ¼" (O) scale! A Kayford F3 B-unit, much like the Haysi RR F7B shown on page 37, switches the King Coal prep plant in this dramatic night scene. David's large home layout, featured in May 2006 *Model Railroader*, was detailed to a degree usually reserved for smaller layouts in terms of both size and scale. The layout had to be dismantled in 2005 because of a move, but David is already deep in the planning stages of an even larger version of the A&O in O scale.

Phil Brooks

At the other end of the scale spectrum, with no evident loss in detail or execution, is Phil Brook's N scale Clinch River RR (above). Here at Big Creek Yard, the CR's main coal marshalling yard, a pair of Geeps pulls an SR boxcar from the freight-house lead as a Mallet lumbers over Mack's Gap viaduct with coal destined for the Southern (see *Model Railroad Planning* 2007).

Steve Sherrill's Shady Grove & Sherrill is a freelanced narrow-gauge coal and lumber line set in West Virginia (see *Model Railroad Planning* 2005). The SG&S is On2½: ¼"-scale models running on the same gauge as HO track. Here second-hand EBT hoppers ride up to Davis Babcock Mine No. 4 above Mabie, W.Va. – a forced-perspective N scale structure. The train will actually terminate in a hidden staging yard.

Bill Miller

The anthracite region

FIVE

A postcard cost but one cent to mail when the color cards above and at the top of page 49 were produced around 1910. The photo on page 49 shows the Hudson Coal Co.'s Marvine Breaker at Scranton, Pa.; another Scranton breaker billed as the "largest in the world" is shown above; the lush greenery is suspect. The map on page 49 shows the extent of the four primary anthracite coalfields, underlying 484 square miles in northeastern Pennsylvania.

Many of the coal beds that once spread over much of the eastern U.S. were long gone by the time today's "new" Appalachians had been folded upward, then eroded down almost to their roots. Plate tectonics compressed and heated the bituminous beds in northeastern Pennsylvania, changing them into rock-hard anthracite coal. By the time someone figured out what hard coal was good for, most of it, along with thousands of feet of rock above it, had eroded away. Only in the bottoms of the folds, the synclines, was some coal left to mine in the northern, east-middle, west-middle, and southern anthracite fields (see **fig. 3** on page 14). (A different mechanism, volcanic heating, created the small anthracite depots found elsewhere in North America.)

Smokeless coal

Anthracite mining would give the typical bituminous-coal miner nightmares. The coal seams are not horizontal, but instead often form a synclinal U shape. The working face of a hard-coal seam was usually high above the miners' feet, and the squeezing pressures that created this metamorphic rock caused faults and variations in the thickness of the coal. Collieries, known as preparation plants in bituminous country, were aptly called *breakers* in the hard-coal region.

The good news is that the seams of coal caught up in these crushing forces were compressed and heated until most of the volatile remnants of their ancestral vegetation were driven out. The result is almost pure carbon. Anthracite releases heat more slowly per square foot of grate area, hence the large Wootten fireboxes on many Eastern railroads' steam power (shown on page 85), but it burns cleaner. Lackawanna's Phoebe Snow with her dress so white, riding on the road of anthracite, made this point to train riders in the pre-air-conditioning era and to home-furnace users alike.

Coal from the anthracite fields was initially transported to market by canal barges, then by the railroads, including the pioneering Delaware & Hudson Canal and then the D&H Railroad. Major eastern carriers – among them Central Railroad of New Jersey; Delaware & Hudson; Delaware, Lackawanna & Western; Erie; Lehigh & New England; Lehigh Valley; New York, Ontario & Western; and Reading – were built to tap into the anthracite region.

The market for hard coal was primary focused on the home-heating industry, as the coal – once ignited – tended to burn without smoke. The iron and steel industry was also a large consumer of hard coal, as was the aluminum industry, where anthra-

Largest Coal Breaker in the World, Electrically operated near Scranton, Pa.

Chuck Yungkurth collection

Anthracite region

Loyalsock coalfield
Northern (Wyoming) coalfields
Bloomsburg
Sunbury
Eastern Middle coalfields
Western Middle coalfields
Allentown
Bethlehem
Southern coalfields
Reading
Harrisburg

MAP AREA
NY
PA
NJ
MD
DE
WV

Tony Koester

cite was used for pot linings and carbon electrodes. It was also used to filter and purify drinking water, to smelt ore, and to make city gas, petroleum products, and chemicals. By-products of hard coal were used to make yarns, toothpaste, face and shaving creams, and even detergents.

The demand for anthracite waned in the 1920s and '30s, as even smokeless coal and automatic stokers were no match for the convenience of oil or natural gas in the home-heating market. Surface mining continued long after the underground operations

ceased. Even the vast piles of culm from the original cleaning process were reclaimed to remove fine anthracite particles suitable for filtration and burning in modern generating plants.

Anthracite vignettes

The following pages feature photos of typical breakers and the railroads that served them. Students of anthracite mining will also enjoy a visit to the Anthracite Museum in McDade Park on Bald Mountain Road in Scranton, Pa., and to the miner's village and museum at Eckley, Pa., where "The Molly Maguires" was filmed.

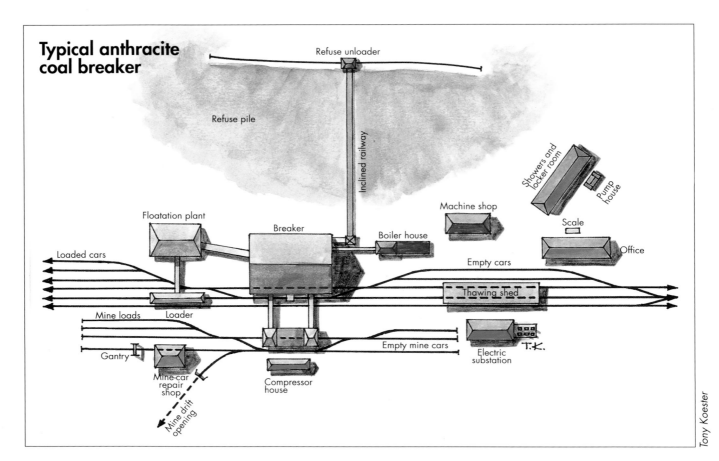

Typical anthracite coal breaker

Refuse unloader

Refuse pile

Inclined railway

Showers and locker room

Pump house

Machine shop

Scale

Office

Floatation plant

Breaker

Boiler house

Empty cars

Loaded cars

Thawing shed

Mine loads

Loader

Empty mine cars

Gantry

Mine-car repair shop

Electric substation

T.K.

Compressor house

Mine drift opening

Tony Koester

This plan of trackwork around a typical breaker was made from a sketch provided by Robert A. Stafford based on his years of experience in the anthracite region. It is not to scale, but it shows the main breaker, associated support buildings, and trackage. The mine is off toward the bottom of the drawing; an inclined railroad moves the culm, or waste material, to nearby piles. Note that run-of-mine coal hauled in from other tipples was thawed (in the winter) and also dumped near the breaker.

Chuck Yungkurth collection

Almost 500 workers were employed at this breaker in Mahanoy (ma-ha-NOY) City, Pa., in 1892. "Modern" steel hopper 88653 at left has P&R (Philadelphia & Reading) reporting marks; the wood car at right seems more in tune with the age of the wood breaker. The sign above the steel hopper appears to read, "No admittance to persons not employed in this building." Anthracite coal came into the colliery along tracks in the covered passageway at the upper right.

The three photos on this page all show breakers typical of those that once dotted northeastern Pennsylvania. This is the Moffat Coal Co. breaker at Taylor, Pa.; its heyday had long passed by the time this photo was taken in August 1976.

The Loree Colliery at Larksville, Pa., was still in limited operation in 1976 using trucks rather than rail to ship coal.

"Blue Coal" was the trademark used by the Huber Colliery, Glen Alden Coal Co., at Ashley, Pa. The photo shows just a small part of this huge complex.

A small "critter" (visible behind the hopper) was being used to move 100-ton hoppers around this breaker in July 1993. Note the scale house and truck scale at right.

Chuck Yungkurth

The size of coal coming out of a mine can be judged by the loaded mine cars evident in the photo at left. The Hudson Coal Co. operations at Olyphant, Pa., employed small steam tank engines to move mine cars around the breaker, as shown in the circa 1956 photo (below left). Below right is an April 1965 photo of another mine "lokey"; this one shuttled mine cars around the Glen Alden Coal Co. breaker at Wanamie, Pa. Note the B&O hoppers in the background, which confirm reports that hoppers from bituminous-coal railroads were reloaded by the anthracite coal companies rather than being returned home empty.

E.L. Thompson

Phil Jubinski; Chuck Yungkurth collecton

Chuck Yungkurth collection

Robert F. Collins

A trio of beefy Delaware & Hudson Consolidations (1208, 1213, and 1217) shove
symbol freight WR-1 out of Carbondale, Pa.,
on Oct. 19, 1951 (above), in a portrait
graphically depicting why housewives who
hung their wash out to dry weren't railfans.
At right, a Lackawanna Geep switches a
colliery that produced the "smokeless"
anthracite made famous by Phoebe Snow.
Many coal-hauling railroads dieselized with
freight units painted in somber black so as to
avoid unduly offending the coal companies
that originated so much of their tonnage.

THIS TAG IDENTIFIES
HUDSON
"The HCCo."
COAL
RE-ORDER BY NAME

S. Botsko

A Central Railroad of New Jersey Alco RS-3 and a pair of Reading Geeps work in the yard between Hauto and Tamaqua, Pa. (above), on a snowy day in February 1971. The "fried egg" herald used by Old Companies Lehigh and the Lehigh & New England is evident on the GE critter switching the Greenwood Breaker (below). A Central of New Jersey RS-3 works at right.

Jim Hertzog collection

Among the smaller anthracite carriers was the Lehigh & New England, which operated a fleet of white-striped black Alco switchers, RS-2s, and FA-1s and FB-1s (above). The herald on the nose showed the railroad's financial ties to owner Old Companies Lehigh. The L&NE's demise in 1961 was as much due to the declining fortunes of the coal company as of the railroad. Below, a former Reading T-1 4-8-4 took a break from fantrip service to switch hoppers on the Blue Mountain & Reading in April 1991. Pockets of the once-sprawling network of coal branches served by the Reading in northeastern Pennsylvania still receive rail service.

Tony Koester

Coalfields in the cornfields

Paul Dolkos

SIX

A leased Chicago, Burlington & Quincy Mikado works Peabody Mine no. 4 on the Bevier & Southern at Binkley, Mo., in October 1962. The B&S delivered coal to the Burlington at Bevier.

It may come as a surprise to those who think of coal mining as being primarily the domain of the central Appalachian states as well as Colorado, Utah, Montana, and Wyoming to discover that most of Illinois is underlain by rich coal deposits. Sixteen of the largest U.S. soft-coal mines in 1971 were in Illinois and Indiana, all but four built since 1950, and if you visit southern Indiana today, you'll see one new coal mine after another.

Almost 32 percent of the tonnage carried by the Burlington in 1913 and again in 1925 was coal and coke. In 1930, a quarter of the always-hustling Wabash's total tonnage and almost 10 percent of its revenue were derived from coal shipments. Across the Ohio River in western Kentucky, Mr. Peabody's coal trains were doing their best to haul away the town of Paradise in Muhlenberg County.

Midwestern coalfields

The Midwest has two main coalfields separated by the Mississippi River. The eastern field comprises medium-volatile bituminous coal deposits that reach from western Kentucky up through southwestern Indiana to cover all but the northern tier of Illinois. The other and considerably larger field, mainly medium-volatile bituminous edged with high-volatile coal along its western border, extends under most of southern Iowa through northwestern Missouri and eastern Kansas to eastern Oklahoma and into a small part of Arkansas. A third coalfield is in central Texas. Oddly enough, central Michigan has both high- and medium-volatile bituminous fields.

Bituminous coal mining in the Midwest followed the national trend by reaching a peak around World War II, then subsiding through the 1960s after steam locomotives were retired and homes and businesses switched to gas and oil heat. In the Winter 1993 issue of *The Banner* (Wabash RR Historical Society), Mark Vaughan reported that by 1960, coal traffic on the Wabash had declined to 11 percent of total tonnage; coal generated only 3.2 percent of its revenues that year, an indication of the drop in on-line coal production.

Then came the oil crisis of the 1970s, which forced electric utilities to take another look at coal. Moribund coal branches of trunk-line railroads have come back to life as regional carriers such as the Indiana Rail Road, the Indiana Southern, and the Algiers, Winslow & Western operate a colorful array of second-hand motive power ranging from first-generation EMD SDs to ex-Southern Pacific tunnel motors still in SP gray and scarlet.

Odd as it may seem to see corn fields rubbing elbows with towering coal-cleaning plants and storage silos, coal production in the midlands is unlikely to decline any time soon.

The top photo shows Fairview Colleries' "modern" Harmattan Mine on the Peoria & Eastern at Hillery, Ill., in September 1952. The middle and bottom photos show mines on the Galesburg & Great Eastern – a 10-mile short line that connected to the Burlington at Wataga, Ill. The middle photo shows Wataga in 1955; the bottom image shows Middle Grove circa 1960.

These three photos show the front and back of the Buckheart Mine at Canton, Ill., served by the Burlington Route, on May 22, 1938. Hoppers and gondolas are both being loaded, and it must have been a warm spring day, as many of the windows are propped open for better ventilation. The Burlington's *Official Freight Shippers Guide and Directory* of the 1930s listed on-line coal mines in Colorado, Illinois, Iowa, Kansas, Missouri, Montana, and Wyoming.

The rustic Big Bend Coal mine at Knoxville, Iowa, was loading out 400 tons of coal per day in July 1977. Knoxville was served by the Burlington Route.

Lloyd Keyser

Bokoshe, Okla., is just west of the Arkansas state line and was originally served by the Fort Smith & Van Buren (Kansas City Southern) and the Midland Valley. These Missouri Pacific hoppers are being loaded at a modern tipple in April 1978.

Lloyd Keyser

Frisco and MoPac offset-side twin hoppers are being loaded at this tipple on the Missouri Pacific north of Rich Hill, Mo., in 1960. The area is now served by a short line.

Lloyd Keyser

Jim Boyd

Jim Boyd

Squaw Creek Coal Co. operations in southern Indiana hosted a number of exotic diesels in the 1970s, including an ex-Santa Fe Alco "alligator" rolling past a Studebaker Lark in May 1977 (top). Peabody Coal operated a number of mines and prep plants using a fascinating mix of Alco (left, at the Lynnville Mine in southern Indiana), Baldwin, and Fairbanks-Morse diesels. Jim Boyd came across the mine at Paradise, Ky., made famous by John Prine's song (bottom left). Remote-controlled switchers were often used to move cars under tipples, this one near Kolbe, Ill. (bottom right).

Jim Boyd

Jim Boyd

Most coal roads originally consumed a lot of the coal they hauled. Here Chicago & Illinois Midland 2-10-2 751 pauses between runs alongside a steel coal dock at Springfield, Ill., in July 1957 in an evocative portrait of coal railroading in the steam era.

Today, coal trains are powered by brightly painted diesels, many of them previously owned, such as SD40s on the Indiana RR (above left), SD24s lettered for Algiers, Winslow & Western on the Indiana Southern (above right), and red-and-gold GPs and slugs on the Indiana Southern (bottom left) where Yankeetown Dock SDs (bottom right) used to tread.

The Burlington was a major mover of Midwestern coal. At left, 2-10-4 6311 leads a string of hoppers at Centralia, Ill., on July 11, 1954. Note the oscillating Mars light housing above the headlight. Today, Burlington successor Burlington Northern Santa Fe continues the tradition of using big power to move heavy coal drags, illustrated at left by C44-9W 5027 on train C-NAMPHH (Coal, North Antelope Mine to Peoria/Havana/ Hennepin, Ill.). The diesel heads down the three-day-old Tazewell & Peoria RR's double-track main approaching Pekin, Ill., on Nov. 3, 2004. The new railroad was formerly the Peoria & Pekin Union; BNSF has trackage rights on the T&P.

Joe Collias; Bill Raia collection

David Jordan

Ted Richardson

Jim Boyd

The Illinois Central was another major coal mover in the Midwest. Here two "Paducah Geeps" (GP7s and GP9s rebuilt at the IC's Paducah, Ky., shops) lug hoppers through Centralia, Ill., in November 1978 not far from where C&IM 751 (page 61) was photographed almost a quarter-century earlier.

The end of the line for coal moving by rail often occurs at a river, one of the Great Lakes, or an ocean port. In May 1977, a Kaskaskia River Port District Geep in a St. Louis-San Francisco-inspired paint scheme moves loads to Dock Facility No. 1 west of Lenzburg, Ill., where the coal will be reloaded into barges.

Paul Fredericoni; courtesy Jerry Glow

CB&Q; Lloyd Keyser collection

Coal was shipped to countless local fuel dealers scattered throughout the Midwest. Lee Freeman built this model of a coal delivery trestle (left) for his Missouri Pacific-inspired HO layout. The photo at right shows a retail coal yard that's about as basic as can be: a gondola full of coal, a conveyor, and a pile of coal awaiting pickup by a local fuel dealer.

David Jordan

What looks like a ballasted staging yard with a power-plant photo pasted on the sky backdrop was taken at the Illinois & Midland's twice-expanded Crescent Yard at Powerton, Ill., in July 2005. At least one UP train arrives from Wyoming each day to supply the Midwest Generation LLC power plant in the background. Another daily UP train is forwarded to Dominion Kincaid's generating station near Sicily, Ill. BNSF trains and power continue to Havana, Ill., to a rail-to-barge transfer or to AmerenIP's power plant.

Coal in the West

Tony Koester

A southbound Rio Grande coal train appears to be coiled like a snake about to strike as it negotiates a curve along the Joint Line between Denver and Pueblo, Colo., in 1985.

The map on page 13 shows that despite the upheaval and subsequent erosion that formed the Rocky Mountains, vast pockets of coal remain in the West, most in a north-south band extending from Arizona and New Mexico up through Colorado and Utah into Wyoming, the Dakotas, Montana, and several Canadian provinces. Even California has coal.

The most active Western mines are those in the Powder River Basin around Gillette, Wyo. The lion's share of Wyoming coal is hauled by the Burlington Northern Santa Fe (BNSF) and the Union Pacific, but coal also continues to be a major source of ton-miles on the former Denver & Rio Grande Western lines in Colorado and Utah, now part of the Union Pacific's empire. In 1996, 14 mines in the southern Powder River Basin produced more than 250 million tons of coal.

Much of the coal near the U.S. and Canadian Rockies is at the bottom of the food chain: subbituminous, lignite, and brown coal. Medium- and high-volatile coal is found throughout Colorado, eastern Utah, and northern New Mexico.

Major coal deposits suddenly end along the western edge of the Rockies. That's because everything west of Elko, Nev., is a series of island arcs (like the Philippines) that were bulldozed up along the western edge of the North American tectonic plate as it pulled away from Africa and sailed west. Those collisions shoved up the Rockies; the ongoing scraping of the westward-moving North American plate against the northerly movements of the Pacific plate created the coastal mountain ranges.

A typical coal road

On the next several pages, we'll take a closer look at a good example of a Western coal road, the Denver & Rio Grande Western. Until the development of the huge coalfields around Gillette, Wyo., Colorado – the West Virginia of the Rockies – led the West in coal production. The Rio Grande, which merged with SP and then UP, tapped the heart of Colorado's bituminous coal fields.

Its original line ran south out of Denver, then west through the Royal Gorge to reach beds of medium- and high-volatile soft coal in western Colorado and eastern Utah. The Moffat Road (Denver & Salt Lake, née Denver & Northwestern) merged into the D&RGW and contributed extensive coal deposits on what became the Craig Branch.

With Alco PAs on the *Yampa Valley Mail*, gold and silver Fs on the *California Zephyr*, 2-8-8-2s or SD40T-2s lugging tonnage over Tennessee Pass, and compact Moffat Road 2-6-6-0s, the Rio Grande is an excellent prototype to model or use as the basis for freelancing.

Frank Keller

The three photos above show (from top) D&RGW 5378 leading three other tunnel motors at Banning, Utah, on the Sunnyside Branch in 1991; EMD SD70 demonstrator 7002 on a coal train on the Craig Branch at Phippsburg, Colo., in 1993; and a Rio Grande coal train at the Ute Generating Station in 1999.

A lone Rio Grande FT stands out in a sea of empty coal gons that will soon be headed back to aptly named Carbon County for loading in this 1950s view of Helper, Utah.

D&RGW 2-8-8-2 3600, with 3607 and 3615 helping, heads up Tennessee Pass with an eastbound 42-car extra with coal for Pueblo on Aug. 15, 1954.

And now for something completely different: A Denver & Intermountain coal train trundles down West 32nd Avenue in Denver in this mid-1940s scene.

If this building complex looks familiar, that's because Edna Mine on the Rio Grande's Craig Branch is the prototype for the popular Walthers New River Coal Co. prep plant kits in HO and N scales. The photo above shows the facility in 1971, and the view below dates from the 1980s; note the new storage silo in the later view. Many Western tipples have a distinctive look (see page 71), but this building could be dropped into Appalachia – as many modelers have done – without raising an eyebrow.

The Utah Ry. connects with and has trackage rights over the Rio Grande. A quartet of gray Alco RSDs has a long string of hoppers in tow near Helper, Utah (above). In later years, the Utah ran ex-Santa Fe Alco "alligators" and then second-hand EMD SD45s, always putting on a spectacular show of horsepower against tonnage and gravity.

At left is a photo of the coal mine at Wattis, located higher than Soldier Summit at 7,600 feet above sea level at the head of a blind canyon.

Jeff Wilson visited the Cordero-Rojo mine and load-out in the Powder River Basin in October 2003. There's nothing about this operation that isn't super-sized, from the shovels and trucks to truck dumps and loading silos. This surface-mining area of Wyoming and Montana has taken over the lead in coal production from the traditional black-diamond mining capitals of West Virginia and eastern Kentucky, tapping seams more than 100 feet thick.

Eric Brooman

Paul Dolkos

An excellent example of a freelanced Western coal hauler is Eric Brooman's HO Utah Belt (above). Eric took this photo of an eastbound UB coal train approaching U.S. Carbon's Mine 26 tipple near Iron Mountain, N.M., a small town just west of the Continental Divide. The tank car visible above the diesels contains fuel for mine machinery. A hallmark of the Utah Belt is Eric's ongoing quest to ensure that the railroad is kept up to date, so – as on the full-size railroads – older motive power and rolling stock are continually being replaced.

The fabled Colorado narrow-gauge lines also tapped into the region's coal seams. Here an eastbound freight picks up coal loads from a Rocky Mountain Fuel Co. tipple near Baldwin on Mary and Bill Miller's On3 Ohio Creek Extension of the Colorado & Southern.

Five rebuilt SD26s up front and four more two-thirds of the way back power this 86-car unit coal train near Topock, Ariz., in October 1974. The train is bound from York Canyon, N.M., to Kaiser Steel in Fontana, Calif. From the opening of the Fontana mill during WWII into the 1970s, coal came from mines on the Denver & Rio Grande Western in Utah. The UP hauled it across Nevada to the Santa Fe at Barstow, Calif., which forwarded the coal over Cajon Pass to San Bernardino. Santa Fe's Kaiser Turn trains moved coal in Rio Grande drop-bottom gons. In the 1960s, Fontana's coal began moving in unit trains made up of D&RGW and UP 100-ton hoppers using pooled power from both roads.

Steve Patterson

This unidentified mine on the Union Pacific, typical of many Western tipples, is loading gondolas instead of hoppers. Note the wood side extensions on the gon in the center.

Union Pacific

Burlington Northern coal train KRO76 is loaded at the Knife River Mine near Gascoyne, N.D., on July 27, 1994. The train will then head for the power plant at Big Stone City, S.D. The mine has since closed owing to the high sulfur content of this coal bed.

Charles Bohi

Black-diamond destinations

Tony Koester

The coal dock at Sunrise, Va., was a destination for several loads of steam coal each day and hence was an important "industry" on the author's HO scale Allegheny Midland.

EIGHT

When we visualize long trains of loaded hoppers headed for market, we tend to think of steel mills and power plants, which are indeed major users of coal. Well into the middle part of the 20th century, however, local retail coal dealers also played a significant role. A dump truck would back up to a basement opening at a home or business, and lumps of coal would clatter down a metal chute into a dusty pile near the furnace. Yet 25 percent of coal production was used to fuel the railroads' steam locomotive fleets, especially in the East and Midwest (oil was often used in the West and Southwest). The coal dock's delivery track is therefore an important industry on a steam-era model railroad, as shown in the above photo.

Moving coal to customers

In the steam and early diesel eras, coal was forwarded much like general freight, in loose car shipments. Just as lumber or perishables are shipped before customers can be found, carloads of coal were often forwarded without bills of lading – "no bills." By the time they reached a major coal marshalling yard, a coal broker had usually found customers, and waybills could be prepared. If not, the coal was stored in the yard.

This is modeled by creating mine bills that specify the type of coal (nut, stoker, lump, etc.) loaded into each car, but not the customer. The loads are then routed to a holding yard. There, the yardmaster digs into a stack of "special" waybills representing orders from customers and matches the desired coal size with what is in the yard. The special waybills are put in car-card pockets in place of the mine tickets, which are returned to the mines for reuse. The loads are then classified and forwarded according to those waybills.

Loose-car coal railroading staggered into the 1960s. Then came the gas crisis of the early 1970s. Suddenly the government was leaning on major petroleum users, such as power plants, to switch to coal. Almost overnight the demand for coal skyrocketed, and solid-coal unit trains became the norm. This is easily modeled using mine-block tickets that list the first and last car numbers and the number of cars in the block.

The accompanying photos show examples of customers of all sizes that depended on timely coal shipments.

The Nickel Plate's ex-Wheeling & Lake Erie coal loader on Lake Erie at Huron, Ohio (top right), was an interim destination for southeastern Ohio coal. The aerial view of Huron (right) shows a grain elevator at left, giant Hulett unloaders used for removing iron ore from lake boats, and (near the top of the photo) the coal loading area.

Courtesy Eric Hirsimaki, Milepost Publishing

Most coal piers employed some type of rotary car dumper to quickly empty hoppers and gondolas. The photo above shows part of the N&W's huge dumper at Lamberts Point, Va. Mike Ritschdorff incorporated a working rotary dumper, built by John Kaspar, on his HO N&W Pocahontas Division layout (left).

Even after the Virginian added catenary over the worst grades out of the coal fields, the electric freight "motors" continued to use coal for fuel as power was generated at this imposing plant near Narrows, Va. A more common destination for coal was commercial power plants; maps of power plant locations appeared in June 2002 (Northeast), January 2003 (Southeast), and October 2003 (West) issues of *Trains* magazine.

The shortline Winifrede in central West Virginia hauled coal from a large mine (top) and small tipples (right) to a Chesapeake & Ohio interchange and to a barge loading facility on the Ohio River (bottom).

Pittsburgh is known as the Steel City owing to numerous steel mills that blanketed the river valleys, seen above in May 1970. Birmingham, Ala., and Wheeling, W. Va., were other steel-making centers.

Thanks largely to the assortment of steel mill kits available from Walthers and parts from Plastruct, modeling a steel mill, like the one Mike Ritschdorff incorporated on his Norfolk & Western layout at Ironton, Ohio, is no longer an onerous task (left).

Steel mills use copious quantities of coke – coal baked but not burned in ovens (top) to drive off the impurities. The ovens were "charged" from the top with coal. Later, the coke was loaded into hoppers (off to the right).

The author built Raymond Brick Co. at Lime Springs on his HO Allegheny Midland to provide a destination for coal to fire the kilns as well as a source of brick and tile carloadings. In the 1950s at Cayuga, Ind., his father managed what is now reportedly the last brickyard in the U.S. still fired with coal.

Tony Koester

Tony Koester

The typical coal silo at left was served by the Chicago & North Western at Norway, Mich. (shown in May 1980). Below left are similar silos at Brandon, Wis. (in May 1982) and, at bottom left, the Bluff City coal yard at Stillwater, Minn., in 1984. The photo below shows a rectangular silo at Monmouth, Ill., in 1989.

Lloyd Keyser

Lloyd Keyser

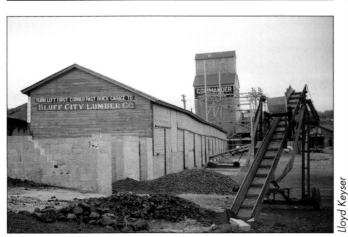

Lloyd Keyser

Lloyd Keyser

The Holleran & Onufrak coal yard in Binghamton, N.Y. (above and right), was still loading coal into dump trucks for local delivery when Chuck Yungkurth visited it in 1984.

An elevated track made it easier to dump coal into a truck-loading conveyor at Brookings, S.D., in 1981.

The N&W hopper was a long way from home when Lloyd Keyser photographed it at a bare-bones coal yard in Scott Lake, Mich., in 1984.

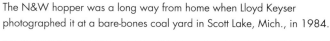

A chain-link fence, siding, conveyor, and (off to the right) scale house make up another simple coal yard, this one shown along the Western Maryland in 1971.

An Alco RS-1 delivers a load of coal to a fuel dealership on *Model Railroader* senior editor David Popp's N scale New Haven layout. The trestle is a Bar Mills kit.

Gene Huddleston

The compound articulated 2-6-6-2 was a coalfield favorite on the Chesapeake & Ohio, which had Baldwin build another ten class H-6 locomotives as late as 1949. Here one of the Class of '49, 1301, rolls through Logan, W.Va., on June 6, 1951.

The articulated compound (Mallet) steam locomotive seems to have been invented to drag coal out of the mountains, with one engineer and fireman operating two engines under a lengthened boiler. For mine runs, the 2-6-6-2 offered a good balance between size and capability; Baldwin's last steam locomotive was a 2-6-6-2 built to old specifications for the Chesapeake & Ohio in 1949. Railroads such as the Norfolk & Western, Virginian, and Rio Grande employed 2-8-8-2s in the coalfields as well as out on the main line. Heavier still were the C&O's Lima-built 2-6-6-6 Alleghenies, super-power locomotives designed to be efficient at high speeds yet, oddly enough, utilized to lug heavy coal trains at relatively slow speeds out on the high iron, as were the nearly identical Blue Ridges on the Virginian. Still other railroads, such as the Louisville & Nashville, employed Mikados and Berkshires to haul coal to market. When diesels came, B-B trucked Alco RS and C-420 units were joined by six-wheel-trucked versions and then "C-boats" from General Electric.

Choosing motive power

A 2-6-6-2 is a nice wheel arrangement for a model coal road. My HO Allegheny Midland had 30"-minimum-radius curves, and larger articulateds such as Challengers and Alleghenies (2-6-6-6s) overhung excessively on those curves. The 2-6-6-2s, on the other hand, seemed right at home.

This is a form of reverse engineering that I should have adopted at the outset. If the whole point of the railroad had been to employ 2-6-6-6s on mainline runs, then I should have run tests to see what radius was needed to allow the engines to look good as well as perform flawlessly. Since I put more focus on coal branch operations, sharper curves could be used to put more railroad in the available space.

In the diesel era, models of the compact Alco RSD-4 and RSD-12 and the EMD SD35 (as compared to an RSD-7 or -15, an SD40, or a U30C) allow for more freight cars in yard, passing, and staging tracks.

"Previously owned" power

The coal rush in the 1970s created a need for more motive power in the coalfields. Eastern Kentucky, for example, became a watering hole for aging Alcos. An already tired fleet of Century 420s off then-parent Seaboard Coast Line joined others from the Tennessee Central and Monon. L&N's big C-628s and C-630s were kept busy pulling and pushing coal trains into Ravenna.

The impact of sound

Visit anyone's model railroad these days and, likely as not, you'll hear a sound-equipped locomotive. In many cases, the engine isn't quite right for the railroad.

Tony Koester

Rebuilt Pacific Fast Mail brass imports of the H-6 2-6-6-2 were the mainstay of mine runs on the author's HO scale Allegheny Midland.

Richard Cook

Other coal roads such as the Norfolk & Western and Wheeling & Lake Erie (Nickel Plate after 1949) also made good use of the 2-6-6-2 wheel arrangement. Here N&W Y5 no. 1411 pauses at Eckman, W.Va., in 1949.

The Virginian and N&W built their physical plants to handle big engines and heavy coal trains. Number 741, one of the Virginian's massive USRA 2-8-8-2s (above), also saw service as N&W 2029 and Santa Fe 1796. The N&W's Y6 2-8-8-2s were among the finest articulateds ever built. Below, class Y6b no. 2180 leads a string of hoppers northbound toward Roanoke on the Shenandoah Division.

But, solely because it offers digital sound, it has joined the roster.

On my new HO railroad, I can test-run DCC sound decoder-equipped locomotives up a steep, twisting grade. Visitors are clearly entranced by the sound of roaring EMD 567-series or Alco 244-series engines or the staccato exhaust of a steam locomotive. Then, halfway up the hill, I hit button 8, shutting off the sound. It's as though the railroad rolled over and died.

I recently operated on Doug Tagsold's spectacular Rio Grande layout, which features the climb out of Denver around Big Ten Curves to Moffat Tunnel and beyond over the former Denver & Salt Lake. Doug uses second-generation EMD and GE power with SoundTraxx sound decoders. As we waited for the power to come on, I noticed that his trains seemed a bit short, a practical solution to the amount of base-ment he had to work with and the number of passing track locations he felt he needed. But when the power was switched on and those EMD turbochargers on a set of GP30 pushers I was assigned to began to sing, I was drawn into the illusion of big-time railroading created by fine modeling and realistic sound.

I have also discovered that engineers take considerably longer to get a train moving with sound turned on than they do with no sound. That's because they carefully jockey the throttle to get just the right blend of movement and engine sounds as they stretch out their trains. They also run trains more slowly so they can hear the power pulses of internal combustion or exhaust beats of steam power.

Thanks to sound, a heavy coal train with helpers strung around the curves of a mountain valley, each and every locomotive mak-ing an audible contribution to the fight against friction and gravity, is finally as aurally awesome as its prototype.

Richard Kindig

The Rio Grande employed 2-8-8-2s as well as 4-6-6-4s to haul tonnage, including coal, around, over, and through the Rocky Mountains. Challenger (4-6-6-4) no. 3702 climbs Soldier Summit near Kyune, Utah, with 47 cars, including coal loads, on June 8, 1947. Engines 3402 and 3509 were pushing.

Leon Stashak

The Delaware & Hudson, like the Clinchfield, was an Eastern coal hauler that employed modern Challenger (4-6-6-4) locomotives to move tonnage over stiff grades. Number 1523 lugs a 4,500-ton train up the mountain near Thompson, Pa., in 1951; two more 1500s were needed as pushers.

David W. Salter

The Virginian bought near copies of Chesapeake & Ohio 2-8-4s and 2-6-6-6s. Class engine no. 900, shown on Feb. 3, 1953, rolls west of Suffolk, Va., with 144 loads of bituminous headed for Norfolk's coal piers.

C. A. Brown

Once the Mallets had trundled out of the mountains with coal loads, Chesapeake & Ohio's fleet Kanawha 2-8-4s took over on the main line. Here no. 2727, near Catlettsburg, Ky., returns empties for mine shifters to distribute in May 1950.

H. Reid

D.H. Noble

Save for the "missing" steam dome (it's inside the sand dome), the Virginian's BA-class 2-8-4s were kissin' cousins of the C&O 2-8-4s. At left, no. 506 leaves Sewalls Point, Va., on a Sunday morning in November 1953. The Louisville & Nashville also used Berkshires, known affectionately as Big Emmas, on mainline coal drags (right), as with no. 1975 at Patio, Ky., in 1949.

Railroads that served northeastern Pennsylvania's anthracite region, such as the Lehigh & New England, also burned the hard coal, which necessitated large-grate-area Wootten-type fireboxes. On smaller camelback engines, only the fireman worked at the rear of the boiler; the engineer sat in a cab that straddled the boiler, as on 2-8-0 no. 154. As engines got larger, there was room for a normal cab at the rear, as on hefty 0-8-0 no. 131.

How the mighty have fallen: Lima-built C&O 4-8-4 613 during a service "run in" after being bumped from passenger to heavy-freight helper service (left). Delaware & Hudson 4-8-4 no. 303 was similarly lugging hoppers as it left Port Henry, N.Y., along the west shore of picturesque Lake Champlain in 1950.

Herbert H. Harwood, Jr.

Tony Koester

The quest for big power continued when diesels took over the chore of moving coal over the mountains. Virginian's Fairbanks-Morse H16-44s and H24-66 Train Masters were delivered in a colorful (for the coalfields) yellow-and-black livery, as shown on H16s 20 and 39 leaving Victoria, Va., in March 1956 (above). Following the Virginian's merger into the N&W in 1959, the big FMs wore drab black but were still handling coal in Virginian hoppers at Mullens and Elmore in 1975 (left).

Allen McClelland

A Virginian & Ohio EMD SD24 in as-delivered paint teams up with a GE U25C in the intermediate paint scheme to move coal eastbound to Afton, Va., on Allen McClelland's original HO scale V&O layout. Allen is now building a new edition of a different division of the V&O in a new home.

The Nickel Plate bumped 2-8-4s from the southeastern Ohio coalfields in 1957 with EMD SD9s (above) and Alco RSD-12s. Chesapeake & Ohio also used six-motor Alco road switchers, then traded them in on EMD SD18s that rode on Alco trucks. At right, no. 1812 leads a quartet of SD18s at Clifton Forge, Va., in October 1963.

The Clinchfield dieselized with EMD F units and Geeps, but second-generation power was primarily EMD SDs and GE C-boats. Below, two SD40s head north out of Dante, Va., in 1974 still wearing gray and yellow.

Two Appalachian coal carriers, the N&W and Virginian, dealt with slow-moving coal drags and long, choking tunnels by stringing catenary over critical parts of their main lines. Above, N&W motors power a coal train at Powhatan, W. Va., in 1949. The Virginian also had square-head boxcabs but supplemented them with streamlined GE cab units, as seen at left. The reign of electric freight motors ended with 3,300-hp rectifier hood units, which later went to the New Haven as E33s. At bottom left, a trio of rectifiers leads a 200-car tidewater coal train at Glen Lyn, Va., in December 1960 not long after the N&W merger.

Chuck Yungkurth

Someone apparently didn't get the lettering-height memo on the Pittsburg & Shawmut at Brockway, Pa., in 1993. The railroad's name predates the adoption of the "h" in Pittsburgh.

Tony Koester

The common rusty triangle on the B&O hopper at right shows where someone set a fire to thaw frozen hopper doors in cold weather.

Tony Koester

Tony Koester

The interiors of black-painted hoppers often look rusty (left), while the interiors of brown-painted hoppers often look black (right).

Modeling coal railroad operations

H. Reid

TEN

It's not just "coal." A careful look inside these Norfolk & Western hoppers at Lamberts Point, Va. (above), in 1967 shows a variety of coal sizes, each one destined for a specific customer. Various grades of model coal loads can simulate this important aspect of coal railroading.

A lot of operating potential exists in a model locomotive and the string of loaded hoppers trailing behind it. David P. Morgan's "Tide 470" (reprinted in chapter 1) provides insights about how the operation of a model railroad can be enhanced as heavy coal trains are blended into the mix of merchandise and passenger trains. The coal in those hoppers may be hundreds of millions of years old, but once it sees the light of day, it may have a pressing date hundreds of miles away – in the hold of a waiting ship, at a steel mill, or at a power plant. Even a carload of stove coal for a local coal and lumber dealer may be as important to waiting customers as a new appliance. Coal won't spoil like produce, but it needs to be kept moving toward market – markets, actually, since the size of the product and its chemistry make each load of coal

Wayne Brumbaugh

Flatland railroads generate operating interest at interchanges located every few miles. Mountain railroads can make up for the lack of such interchange traffic with numerous lineside coal tipples and helper and pusher locomotives moving heavy coal trains out of the mountains. The Western Maryland used as many as eleven big Consolidations (2-8-0s) to move a single coal drag out of Elkins, W.Va., to the main line at Cumberland, Md.

as different as a carload of clothes washers is from a load of dryers or refrigerators.

Coal loads both ways

On my Allegheny Midland, as on the Chesapeake & Ohio, coal that was headed east to tidewater ports along the Atlantic coast was called *tide* coal. Coal headed north toward the steel mills and power plants that rim the Great Lakes was dubbed *lake* coal. As a result, when a mine run or shifter rolled back down a branch to the junction with the main line, tide coal would be set out in the junction yard for pickup by the next southbound coal drag. Lake coal continued north to the division point at South Fork, W.Va., for forwarding on a coal drag or freight train.

The coal was sorted into more than those two classifications, however. The coal preparation plant and mine at Big Springs, W.Va. (page 95), had four tracks under the tipple. Each track "loaded out" a specific size of coal,

with the smallest coal, *slack*, loaded out first in the track nearest the mine-shaft elevator's tower. The other tracks typically loaded out nut, steam or stoker, and lump. Each size of coal was billed to a different customer, with six to eight cars per day routed to the AM's coal docks at South Fork, W.Va., and Sunrise, Va., to replenish the tenders of the Midland Road's steam fleet.

This underscores an important point, one I discussed in my book *Realistic Model Railroad Operation* (Kalmbach Publishing, 2003): Engine terminals are important customers or industries on a model railroad. Steam locomotives require considerable quantities of coal or fuel oil as well as sand to spread out on the railheads in front of their drivers. Diesels need fuel and sand.

On the AM, coal originated primarily on the Otter Creek and Coal Fork subdivisions. In addition to the mine and prep plant at Big Springs, kitbashed from a Walthers New River Mining Co. kit (available in both HO and N; page 95), there was a single-track tipple there based on a prototype I spotted at Roaring Fork on the Clinchfield (page 37), a truck dump (page 96) and three-track tipple at Coal Fork (page 36), and a two-track tipple at Low Gap that was kitbashed to resemble a mine owned by Republic Steel at Republic, Ky. (pages 34 and 93). Another pair of kitbashed tipples was located at Big Springs Junction (page 93), where the OC branch joined the main line. Most of these tipples were described in the October 1998 issue of *Model Railroader*.

David Stewart (above) can get up close and personal with trains operating over his O scale Appalachian & Ohio, a freelanced railroad unrelated to the new A&O that operates some former B&O coal lines in West Virginia. See page 46 for another photo of the spectacular A&O, which is being replaced by an even larger edition. Mike Ritschdorff is another modeler who enjoys big-time coal railroading in his basement (left). Mike models the Norfolk & Western and other Pocahontas roads in HO. The massive coal prep plant was built by John Kaspar. John's rotary coal dumper is shown on page 74.

AM mine runs

As the day began, the Low Gap Shifter behind a 2-6-6-2 Mallet had completed its work above Low Gap (an unmodeled section of the branch) and was already headed down the branch past the Wheeling Steel tipple at Low Gap (page 93, bottom right). It continued down the branch, left tide coal loads at Big Springs Junction, and headed for the barn at South Fork. That evening, the

Low Gap Shifter gathered up empties and headed back up to Low Gap and beyond.

During the day, the Otter Creek Shifter (powered by another 2-6-6-2) was called at South Fork (page 93, top). It rounded up the day's quota of empty hoppers, ran up Cheat River Grade to Big Springs Junction, worked the tipples there (page 93, bottom left), then headed up the Otter Creek Sub to Big Springs, where it

shoved its empties through the bypass track beside the prep plant, then pulled the loads (page 95). It also worked the Roaring Fork loader before returning to BJ, doing more work if needed, setting out tide coal, and running back home with lake coal.

Not far behind and perhaps even ahead of the Otter Creek Shifter was the Coal Fork Shifter, which also headed up the Otter Creek Subdivision to Big Springs,

South Fork on the author's HO Allegheny Midland (above) was the home of the 2-6-6-2 Mallets that worked the coal fields. The Otter Creek Shifter worked the tipples at Big Springs Junction (bottom left) and Big Springs, W.Va., while the Low Gap Shifter theoretically worked tipples beyond Low Gap (bottom right). Another mine run, the Coal Fork Shifter, worked tipples between Coal Fork and Low Gap.

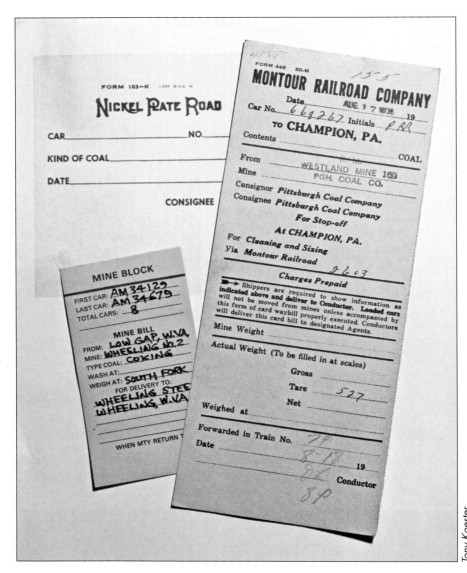

FORM 103-K 10M 8-64 H

Nickel Plate Road

CAR_____ NO._____

KIND OF COAL_____

DATE_____

CONSIGNEE

MINE BLOCK

FIRST CAR: AM 34-129
LAST CAR: AM 34-679
TOTAL CARS: 8

MINE BILL

FROM: LOW GAP, W.VA.
MINE: WHEELING No.2
TYPE COAL: COKING
WASH AT:
WEIGH AT: SOUTH FORK
FOR DELIVERY TO:
WHEELING STEEL
WHEELING, W.VA

WHEN MTY RETURN T

FORM 448   50-M

MONTOUR RAILROAD COMPANY

Date AUG. 17 1976   19___

Car No. 669267   Initials P.RR.

to CHAMPION, PA.

Contents _____ COAL

From   WESTLAND MINE 16
Mine   PGH. COAL CO.

Consignor Pittsburgh Coal Company
Consignee Pittsburgh Coal Company
For Stop-off

At CHAMPION, PA.

For Cleaning and Sizing
Via Montour Railroad

Charges Prepaid

➤ Shippers are required to show information as indicated above and deliver to Conductor. Loaded cars will not be moved from mines unless accompanied by this form of card waybill properly executed. Conductors will deliver this card bill to designated Agents.

Mine Weight _____

Actual Weight (To be filled in at scales)

Gross _____

Tare   527

Net _____

Weighed at _____

Forwarded in Train No. 74

Date   8-17   19___

Conductor

Mine paperwork was as varied as the mines themselves. Montour RR Form 448 routed cars from Pittsburgh Coal Co.'s Westmoreland Mine 16 to the cleaning and sizing plant at Champion, Pa. The Nickel Plate Form 103-K simply specified the car type and number, kind of coal, and date as well as the consignee. The Old Line Graphics mine bill makes it simple to route one or more cars in a block to a specific destination – a preparation plant or a customer.

Tony Koester

then continued into the hollers via the Coal Fork Subdivision to work tipples near Coal Fork.

The Allegheny Midland's main line was controlled by CTC, but the coal subdivisions were "dark" – that is, unsignaled. The AM dispatcher at South Fork therefore had to dictate train orders and issue a Clearance Form A to each crew (there wasn't enough such work to keep an operator busy) when they left the main at Big Springs Junction.

Staging the railroad

At the actual prep plant at Summerlee, coal was mined deep underground and hoisted to the surface for cleaning and sizing. But nearby, another tipple on the C&O had no preparation facilities, so the C&O delivered this raw or cleaner coal to the Virginian at a small yard at Carlisle, W.Va.

The Virginian used a Fairbanks-Morse Train Master to haul the coal to the Summerlee prep plant, where it was shoved around behind the plant to the yard where empties for loading were stored. This cleaner coal was then routed to a car shaker (used to free frozen coal; see page 95, middle) and dumped into a pit. A conveyor elevated it to the top of the prep plant to the same point where deep-mine coal was dumped.

So to some extent, this was a loads-in/loads-out operation, and

Although he enjoys operating the railroad realistically, Rob Enrico designed his O scale edition of the Pennsylvania RR's Monongahela Division specifically to allow him to shoot photos of scenes he had admired in his youth, as he described in *Model Railroad Planning 2006*. Here a coal train rumbles past the West Brownsville, Pa., depot. Equipment changes allow him to depict eras from late steam through second-generation diesels.

Rob Enrico

both C&O and Virginian hoppers could be found under the prep plant. I copied this practice at Big Springs by routing some loaded hoppers from truck dumps to the prep plant. They were all old hoppers marked with a big yellow circle to warn against interchanging them and hence dubbed *yellow balls*, a term and practice I picked up from the Louisville & Nashville.

I made no attempt to have removable loads in my hopper cars, as the huge number of different types of double-, triple-, and four-bay hoppers from various manufacturers would have made matching loads to hopper types a maddening exercise. By the end of an operating session, most loaded hoppers had been moved into north- or south-end staging yards, and empties had been spotted under the tipples. Between sessions, I ran the coal trains back to the tipples and took the empties to the classification or staging yards. I also removed loaded cars from the coal docks in the engine terminals and replaced them with empties.

This took a few hours, but I got to run the railroad myself for several hours each month, something I rarely got to do during operating sessions. I enjoyed seeing trains pass through the Alleghenies while checking out the railroad to be sure there were no unreported track, electrical, or equipment problems.

Loaded hoppers were routed either by individual waybills to retail customers or in blocks of cars to major destinations (see the form at the top of page 94). Empties were routed to mines based on empty-car orders, much as empty boxcars could be routed to grain elevators. The forms I used are available from Old Line Graphics, 1504 Woodwell, Silver Spring, MD 20906, and from Micro-Mark, 340 Snyder Ave., Berkeley Heights, NJ 07922-1595 (www.micromark.com).

Tony Koester

Tony Koester

Tony Koester

The Lochgelly mine and prep plant at Summerlee, W.Va., was switched by the Virginian (later N&W) using an FM Train Master and later an ex-NKP SD9 (top). Coal came vertically out of the ground on an elevator under the huge bull wheels. Note the hoist house at right and mine support timbers in the foreground. In the winter, a shaker (middle) was used to dislodge frozen coal brought in from a nearby mine on the C&O. The author kitbashed Walthers New River Mine kits to closely resemble the Lochgelly mine (bottom).

Chuck Yungkurth

Tony Koester

Tony Koester

When space precludes modeling a large mine or prep plant, a small truck dump can generate several carloads of coal per day. Chuck Yungkurth built and photographed a simple loader using a conveyor for his Bellefonte & Snowshoe RR (top). The author kitbashed an Accurail (now Rix) wood overpass to resemble a truck dump on the narrow-gauge East Broad Top (middle); Steve Esposito built the coal truck. Miners may be able to walk to work from a nearby coal camp (company town), or they may need to ride miners' trains up the hollers to reach the tipple. Short passenger trains – the EBT added a coach to the rear of a coal train, giving it a mixed-train-daily appearance – or gas-electrics handled this chore, as shown above on the author's Coal Fork Subdivision of the Allegheny Midland. Such trains, which were sometimes listed as first-class trains in the timetable, add variety to operating sessions.

Helpers vs. interchanges

Mountain railroads tended to follow narrow valleys cut by streams, so crossings with other railroads at grade were few and far between. The traffic generated by interchanges every few miles on flatlands railroads is therefore largely forfeited when modeling a mountain coal railroad. A way around this is to model one of the Midwestern coal roads, which crossed numerous "foreign" railroads on their way from mine to market.

Those who cannot resist the allure of the mountains need another approach to enhance operations and extend runs on their model railroads. Coal railroads offer solutions to both concerns: The steep grades and sharp curves impose speed restrictions, and the need to stop to add helpers on the head-end or at mid-train or to couple pushers onto the rear slows the pace. Retainers need to be turned up at the tops of grades to bottle up some of the air in the braking system to prevent runaways, and a stop has to be made at the bottom of the hill to turn the retainers back down again.

Traffic abounds at tipples along the main and the myriad branches among the hills. Whether you model the plodding shifters gathering coal from the tipples or cope with the mix of higher-speed manifest freights and passenger trains as they encounter coal drags – as Morgan described in "Tide 470" – there is a lot of drama and sheer work to model on a coal road.

Fortunately for coal-railroading enthusiasts, as for the coal and railroad industries, the coal stampede of the 1970s has continued unabated into the 21st century. Security concerns have made it unwise to visit railroad or coal company property without permission, but the magic of big engines working hard to convey coal to customers will continue well into the future.